The MARINE *Quarterly*

A JOURNAL OF THE SEA

NUMBER THIRTEEN

SPRING 2014

Sailing

Published by
The Marine Quarterly Ltd
The Hope, Lyonshall
Kington
Herefordshire HR5 3HT UK

Telephone +44 (0)1544 340636
Email editor@marinequarterly.com
www.marinequarterly.com

ISSN 2045-8959

Editor Sam Llewellyn

The Marine Quarterly is published
on 1 March, 1 June, 1 September and 1 December.
Annual subscription rates (4 issues):
UK £40 Europe £45 Rest of world £55

Design and typesetting by Five Seasons Press
Hereford UK
www.fiveseasonspress.com

Printed by Graficascems, Polígono Industrial
San Miguel 31132 A (Navarra) Spain
and ABC Print (Hereford) Ltd
Moreton-on-Lugg, Herefordshire HR4 8DP UK

All illustrations by Claudia Myatt
except the portrait of Ray Doggett by Guy Venables

Colophon by Simon Dorrell

CONTENTS

Sailing Sam Llewellyn 5

Flotsam and Jetsam 7

Notes from a Svalbard Diary Emma Beynon 14

Rank Amateurs Fraser Fraser-Harris and John Clegg 27

Childhood Sailing in the Fifties John Simpson 39

Downriver with the Lightermen Bob Harris 45

The 1945 Cowes to Dinard Race Nigel Sharp 56

Hammond Innes: a Memoir John Lang 62

The 'Mary Deare' Hammond Innes 66

The Instruments of Navigation Christopher Schüler 79

How to Smoke a Herring Mike Smylie 87

Scilly Pioneers Amanda Martin 94

Salmo Martin Llewellyn 101

From the Editor's Shelf 105

Contributors 110

Cover artists 112

COVER PAINTINGS:

FRONT *A Cunarder being converted to a Merchant Cruiser,*
Herbert Barnard John Everett, oil on canvas, 1918

BACK Detail from *Tabula Rogersiana,* Muhammad al-Idrisi, 1154
NB this map is drawn north downwards, and should be inverted
to be read by modern navigators

Sailing

This is the thirteenth issue of the Marine Quarterly, and I am writing the introduction on a Friday. Neither of these factors is conducive to good fortune. To make the omens even less auspicious, hardly any of this issue's stories contain a working marine engine. But voyages have to start somewhere: so off we go, throwing salt over the left shoulder, pouring a dose of rum into the sea and hoping for a breeze aft of the beam.

We kick off in dangerous waters, joining Emma Beynon, a writer of startling freshness and enthusiasm, on an attempted circumnavigation of Svalbard in an ancient Bristol Channel pilot cutter. To warm up after this icy experience, full of calving glaciers and hungry polar bears, we take some time out in the West Indies, with the funloving veterans of WWII at sea who first noticed that a living could be made, and a life lived, taking people sailing in beautiful but unreliable boats in reliably sunlit and breezy waters.

The North Sea in the 1950s makes a sharp contrast to the Caribbean, but that is where John Simpson did his early sailing, with a family reminiscent of the one that peoples the Giles cartoons of the time. The same horizontal rain and fierce tides were the native atmosphere of the Thames lightermen, a highly skilled body of men who used the tides and a couple of oars to weave fifty-ton cargoes through the intricate mooring trots and traditions of the Port of London in its prime. Nigel Sharp tells the story of a gale-lashed Dinard race, conducted in the year the war ended in an English Channel still studded with mines.

Rear-Admiral John Lang, sometime chief of the UK Government's Marine Accident Investigation Branch, was a lifelong friend of the great sea writer Hammond Innes, who left his royalties to fund sail training for young people. Lang introduces a significant passage from Innes's *The Wreck of the 'Mary Deare'*, just republished and undimmed by the passage of time. I had forgotten the fierceness with which he could ratchet up tension in his storytelling.

So much for adventure on the high seas. We sail into calmer waters with Chris Schuler, an expert on charts and navigational instruments, who gives a lucid account of the development of navigation from the earliest times. Gastronomy next, with a splendid ramble through the herring fisheries and their products, smoked and flapping, from Mike Smylie, alias the Kipperman. We take a trip to Scilly to meet photographers like the extraordinary Gibson dynasty, who with their unwieldy plate cameras braved the foulest Atlantic weather to capture images of shipwrecks and island life. And finally, we follow a salmon parr out of a Canadian river and into the North Atlantic gyre, and reach some disturbing conclusions about its present and future.

As I said, there is hardly a working engine among the lot. On we sail regardless.

Sam Llewellyn

Flotsam and Jetsam

Remarks on the Use of the Lead Line

'Every vessel should have some plank in her deck, marked at every fathom, from one to five, purposely for marking her lead lines. The hand lead line in moderate sized vessels is usually twenty-five fathoms in length, but in large and lofty vessels thirty fathoms.

'When heaving the hand lead you are generally placed outside of the rigging, standing either on the rail, or sheer pole, with a broad canvas belt round your waist, so that you can stretch your body well outside the rail. Take hold of the line about ten feet from the lead, then swing the lead backwards and forwards a couple of times, keep your arm very stiff, then swing it right over your head twice, let go the lead, and give out the line.

'If the lead is well hove, it will drop close alongside the vessel well forward. As the line comes plumb up and down, tap the ground with it smartly, and call out the depth of water. If it is five fathoms, you call out, *By the mark five*. If it is four, you call out, *By the deep four,* and so on; consequently in twenty fathoms of line there are eleven deeps, and nine marks, or in other words, in nine places the line is marked, and in eleven places it is unmarked.

'A good leadsman is not made in a day, and it requires incessant practice for months to be able to heave out twelve fathoms of straight line, in the port channels, and get an eight fathom cast properly. Commence learning to swing the lead with a seven-pound one, and when you find you can swing this well, go in for the fourteen-pound lead, and *mind your head.*

'In former days if a merchant seaman wished to join the Navy, the first order he received from the lieutenant in charge of the deck was, "Go into the port-chains, my lad, and give me a cast of the lead." This shows that being a good leadsman was the first test that authorities in the Navy judged a seaman by.'

From 'Practical Seamanship', 1904, found by Graham Faiella

The Smell of the Land

On the 15th October we encounter'd a little foule weather, which made us creep terra, terra, as they call it, and so a vessell that encounter'd us advised us to do; but our patron, striving to double the point of Savona, making out into the wind put us into great hazard, for blowing very hard from land betwixt those horrid gapps of the mountaines, it set so violently as rais'd on the sudden so great a sea that we could not recover the weather-shore for many houres, insomuch that, what with the water already enter'd, and the confusion of fearful passengers (of which one who was an Irish Bishop, and his brother, a priest, were confessing some as at the article of death) we were almost abandon'd to despaire, our pilot himselfe giving us up for lost. And now, as we were weary with pumping and laving out the water, almost sinking, it pleas'd God on the suddaine to appease the wind, and with much ado and greate perill we recover'd the shore, which we now kept in view within halfe a league in sight of those pleasant villas, and within scent of those fragrant orchards which are on this coast, full of princely retirements for the sumptuousness of their buildings and noblenesse of the plantations . . . from which the wind blowing as it did might perfectly be smelt the peculiar joys of Italy in the perfumes of orange, citron, and jasmine flowers for divers leagues seaward.

From John Evelyn's Diary, 1644

Henry V Heads for France

Suppose that you have seen
The well-appointed King at Hampton pier
Embark his royalty; and his brave fleet
With silken streamers the young Phoebus fanning:
Play with your fancies, and in them behold
Upon the hempen tackle ship-boys climbing;
Hear the shrill whistle which doth order give
To sounds confused; behold the threaden sails,
Borne with th' invisible and creeping wind,
Draw the huge bottoms through the furrow'd sea,
Breasting the lofty surge. O! Do but think
You stand upon the rivage and behold
A city on th' inconstant billows dancing;
For so appears this fleet majestical,
Holding due course to Harfleur.

William Shakespeare

North Sea News

Scotland's Sustainable Inshore Fisheries Trust (SIFT) has accused the Scottish Government of kowtowing to the demands of commercial fishery interests while ignoring the public interest. Commercial scallop dredging and trawling operations inside the twelve-mile limit have almost destroyed stocks of herring and cod in some areas, notably the vast Firth of Clyde, says SIFT. Recreational sea angling, traditional shellfish creeling (lobster potting) and scallop diving have all suffered from constant seabed degradation. Crucial links in the food chain are being weakened and in some cases destroyed.

Things will not get any better until the Scottish Government sorts out the management structure of the Inshore Fishery Groups responsible for the devastation. Historically, IFGs in

Scotland, unlike their English equivalents, have been structured to favour the larger commercial fishing operations. 'The interests of the commercial trawling and dredging sector are never likely to produce management proposals that genuinely serve the public interest', says SIFT Chairman Robert Younger.

Younger believes the Scots have plenty to learn from the English Inshore Fisheries and Conservation Authorities, which are managed as a public resource by a cross section of the public – tourism entrepreneurs, sustainable small-boat fishermen, diving outfits – rather than by vested interests and their big battalions.

'Scotland's IFGs typically exclude everyone except commercial fishermen, and they are dominated by the mobile fleet. This is no way to manage a public asset. Overfishing and the use of fishing gears which damage habitats have not only been permitted but promoted.'

At a recent Scottish Government inshore fisheries review, SIFT has demanded management structure changes and a three-mile limit excluding trawlers and dredgers.

SIFT has also pointed to the massive underfunding of IFGs. Although Scotland's 11,500-mile coastline is twice the length of England's, England's ten Inshore Fisheries and Conservation Authorities (IFCAs) have a combined annual budget of more than £8.6 million, and access to three Royal Navy offshore patrol vessels.

In contrast, direct expenditure by Scotland's twelve Inshore Fisheries Groups is £2 million a year, with access to two occasional planes, the odd RIB in summer, and three mini-frigates used mainly for offshore enforcement.

The SNP-dominated Government is in a tricky position. It wants to keep the commercial fishing industry onside, especially this year, when Scotland votes on the independence issue. On the other hand it spends a great deal of time preaching equal access for all on land. So why not at sea?

The number of reported North Sea oil and chemical spills in 2013 was the lowest for three years. But three of the biggest operators still managed to notch up nearly two hundred spills between them. Step up Shell, heading the dismal championship with eighty-five incidents. Next on the murderboard is Chinese National Offshore Oil Corporation's Nexen with sixty. Bringing up the rear are BP, with a highly discreditable fifty, Talisman Sinopec with a plucky but stinking thirty-eight and Perenco, squeaking into the hall of ill fame with twenty-seven.

Professional seafarers are unprepared to deal with increasing piracy on the high seas. So says skipper Joe Westland, a veteran of the Second Icelandic Cod War who was taken hostage from his oilfield supply vessel off Nigeria late last year.

Westland's experience has left him traumatised and unable to work – hardly surprising, considering that his captors threatened to burn him alive unless his employers coughed up £750,000. They eventually settled for £50,000, but not before Westland had contracted malaria.

'A lot of people go out there [to Nigeria] to work and they don't know what they are getting in to', says Westland. He includes himself in this. He had been working in Nigeria on supply boats for eleven years without incident when he was kidnapped.

> It only takes once. It messes up your whole life. I would not advise anyone to go there. I have faced hardship at sea and tough weather conditions as a skipper. I have been driven by the need to look after my vessel and crew. But nothing prepares you for being kidnapped by pirates and held at gunpoint.

Will salmon decide the outcome of this year's referendum for Scottish independence? Probably not. But disgruntled chunterings on salmon fishing websites suggest that coastal netting on the east coast and fish farms on the west may be issues, if not deciding factors.

In January there was a concerted web campaign to have the First Minister Alex Salmond booed when he turned up to open the Tay salmon fishing season, a ghastly tartan extravaganza made up largely of men in beards with bagpipes at which the guest of honour is required to throw perfectly good whisky into the Tay by way of a pagan oblation to the spirit of the river. The former newsreader Fiona Armstrong, now Lady Macgregor, occasionally lends tone to this otherwise freezing ceremony. Even more occasionally a fish is hauled from the Tay grue (ice floes), only to be thrown back in the name of conservation.

The reasons for the boos are twofold. Firstly, fish farms, heavily promoted by Salmond as the answer to west highland employment woes, are credited with wiping out stocks of wild salmon and sea trout in the west of Scotland. Secondly, the SNP Government's pusillanimous attitude to salmon netting at sea on the east coast is considered a major threat to wild stocks. The salmon netsmen's decision to ditch a voluntary ban on early season netting is being laid entirely at Salmond's door, even though he has no legislative power to change things.

Salmon netting rights are legal rights originating in the Dark Ages, if not earlier. To scrap them would require at least an Act of Parliament. On the other hand, netting mixed stocks of salmon at sea without knowing which rivers they belong to is a complete no-no under EU conservation law. Not very oddly, it is a part of the law that the Scottish Government studiously ignores, because it likes to be seen as the champion of horny-handed netsmen rather than soft-palmed anglers, and to hell with the fish, which do not vote.

Perhaps Scottish independence will prove, in the end, to be the salmon's best chance of survival. Adhering to EU habitat directives will be a key condition of an independent Scotland joining Europe, and the boys in Brussels will be watching closely.

In the spirit of encouragement, rather than enforcement, the Scottish Fishermen's Federation has been offering fishermen free lifejackets – only to discover that the ungrateful toilers of the deep don't want them. The takeup of the one thousand or so on offer has been derisory, and now there are mutterings that if the fishermen won't save themselves someone else will have to do it, forcibly, by legislation.

Refusal to wear lifejackets even when they are available is by no means exclusive to the Scots. The ancient legend that fishermen seldom learnt to swim, on the basis that it was better to drown immediately than flail hopelessly for hours, may or may not have a basis in fact. It is, however, a fact that fishermen have argued that even the modern lifejackets on offer are too bulky to work in – though there is a suspicion that few have tried them to find out.

What is extraordinary is not that Scots are turning down a free gift of some value (though that is odd enough in itself) but that in an age when the passing of wind outside the home is judged a reckless act of industrial pollution, Health and Safety legislation does not ruthlessly enforce a measure widely regarded as perfectly sensible.

Alastair Robertson

Notes from a Svalbard Diary

Emma Beynon

I am sitting below decks on *Dolphin*, at 38′ the smallest surviving Bristol Channel Pilot Cutter, built in Porthleven by J Bowden in 1909. She is a sturdy and forgiving sail, though heavy on the helm. We are moored at the old Gamleka quay in Longyearbyen, the only town in Svalbard, replenishing our provisions. At 78°3′N and 15°37′E we are less than 1000 miles from the North Pole.

Our aim is to circumnavigate the archipelago if the ice allows. Failing that, we intend to sail as far north as we can before we meet the pack ice. Our route was last charted in 1934, with soundings taken more than four miles apart. We really will be nosing into the unknown. The skipper, Roger Capps, has nailed a copper skirt to *Dolphin*'s larch-on-oak hull. This gives her a jaunty air, but we all know that any old growler could make a nasty hole. Moored up against the cruise ships and steel-hulled yachts in the harbour, *Dolphin* looks almost too much of a veteran to withstand this harsh environment. A significant number of locals are amazed at her diminutive size and basic facilities. We talk of Tilman and plum duff.

Yesterday in the bright polar night the harbourmaster saw a polar bear climb into the cockpit of a neighbouring yacht, before wandering off up the dark and dusty mountain behind the town. According to the locals only the young polar bears attack humans. The older ones are just curious.

I can hear the skipper on deck talking to a fellow sailor about the ice. The Norwegian Meteorological Institute in Tromsø produces fabulously detailed computer charts. We do not have the technology to receive such information. We will glean all the ice and weather reports we can in Longyearbyen, after which we will rely on our judgment. I am stowing the provisions and topping up the water in the tanks in the saloon. I had better look sharp.

Friday 18 July: at 1800 hours we slip our mooring and sail to Trygghama at the mouth of Isafjord. 2300, 78°13.3′N, 14°E. It took quite some time to find a safe anchorage at the foot of the glacier. The water is beige and sticky with silt. We tried to anchor in three different places. I am rather worried. We are too close to the glacier. It might calve during the night, and we could be engulfed by a surge of water or ice. *Den Norske Los – Arctic Pilot* is consulted. 'Melting glacier ice is easily recognised by a cracking sound like burning juniper', it says. Can I hear the sound of burning juniper? No. So all is well.

Monday 21 July, Eidenbukta, 78°16′N, 12°48′E: we have spent the last two days trying to sail up Forlandsundet, the channel between Prins Karl Foreland and the mainland, but there was a northwesterly right on the nose, whipping up the shallow water (little wonder that during the seventeenth century it was known as Foul Sound). After an hour on the helm, I become seasick, damp, cold and haunted by the constant lurch of the boat. Luckily the rest of the crew are pleased to have a blast on the helm. Spend the first day and the day after that sleeping. Finally the skipper decides we should hole up on the north side of Eidenbukta Bay.

The anchor keeps dragging. We put down two, and row ashore to take a closer look at the ugly walrus lounging on the beach.

It is a hard row against the wind, and harder still to walk along the silty grey beach. But there they are in a great inert heap, prone and snoring on the pebbles. They are enormous and grimy, their wrinkled brown skin freckled with warts and scars, and they stink of horse muck. Every now and then one of them rears its head, gives a long slow yawn and falls back lifeless into the tangle of blubbery bodies. Sometimes one of them lumbers slowly towards the water, the heat from the exertion turning its skin pink. When they become excessively pink they collapse into a deep sleep until they cool down, turn from pink to brown and start to shuffle on their way once more. Is the collective noun for walrus a cabinet? It is now too cold to reflect on this further.

Back to the boat. Will is fitting the door between the saloon and the cabin. I clean the heads and Tig cleans the kitchen while Capps tightens the rigging. The swell makes the rum bottles chink. At last there is silence. All you can hear is the hiss of the stove.

Tuesday 22 July: Capps raised ten metres of the anchor chain, I did ten metres, then Will brought up the last ten metres and the second anchor, which really was well fastened and covered in silt. A walrus emerged, sighed, gave us a quick glance, then slid beneath the surface. We motored into the Forlandsundet with a light northeasterly behind us.

There are no winches on *Dolphin*, just purchases. Tig and I put up the sails. We bowl along at 8 knots. By early afternoon we arrive at Seelvagen Harbour, 78°33′N, 11°16′E. A splendid steep walk up the ridge above the harbour until we can see a line of snow-capped peaks running up the west side of the channel. Across the clear blue water on the eastern side the mountains are smooth, ground down by the gleaming white glaciers. Every now and then you can hear the deep rumble, almost a moan, of the ice calving. We will be sailing there tomorrow to collect shale samples for Southampton University.

Wednesday 23 July 2009, 1400: bobbed and skipped across Forland Sundet on our way to Hornbaeck-bukta to find the exact spot marked on the Southampton University map. The water off the glacier is uncharted. We edge nervously towards the huge grubby snout, faulted like an accordion. We are negotiating our way through its debris, a mass of 3/10 ice with blocks up to ten yards square, lapped by the water into delicately curved shapes like enormous chandeliers, vases, even a sofa. A freezing wind blows down from the glacier. Will and I are deputised to find the rock samples. We row ashore and walk across a marshy spit that lies to the north of the glacier. Beyond the rocky ridge that contains the glacier the glacial melt just thunders over the dark smooth rocks. Back on board with our samples it is anchor up, and we motor in the midnight sun to Comfortless Cover at Englesbukta (78°50′N, 11°44′E).

0130 hours: Tig is on the helm, Capps and Will are calculating our position with a sextant, I am in my bunk next to the gun in its bright dayglo orange cover, in case of polar bears.

26 July, Hamburgbukta, 79°28.5′N, 10°57′E: 'In calm weather there is excellent anchorage here for smaller vessels. During the whaling period, the bay was used as a base, and later also by other hunters.' (*Den Norske Los* 1990: 270)

When we anchor a harbour seal pops its head above the clear water as if in greeting. Now, three hours later, three seals are lying on boulders by the shore staring at us. The air is seething with the endless chatter of little auks. There is a colony on the southern side of the cove. The sky is positively darkened by the countless flocks circling above our heads.

27 July, Hamburgbukta: catapulted out of bed, through breakfast and onto the glacier. Find ourselves walking over great piles of glacial moraine. The snow on the glacier is soft. Ice further up the slope is melting in the sun, sending great torrents of water

down on us. In an attempt to keep dry Will wraps polythene bags secured with duct tape around his legs. As we approach the peak of the corrie, the little auks dive-bomb us in formation. We make for one of the gullies amongst the coronet of peaks, scrambling over 45° scree slopes at 600′. The rock glints with feldspar, sharp, unweathered, difficult to negotiate. Capps ropes me up. This possibly false sense of security gives me extra energy. I have an easy time of it as I walk up the steps of impacted ice.

Lunch at the col on top of the corrie overlooking Magdalena Fjord. Moss as my plate and three curious auks peering over a ledge watching us eat. To north we look down the western arm of a giant glacier called Gullybreen. From our high position it looks a relatively easy walk down over the snowy glacier into Magdalena Fjord. It is decided that Tig and I are to follow the route we have identified. Capps and Will will return to *Dolphin* and sail around to Magdalena Fjord and meet us there.

Tig and I start our descent into Magdalena Fjord. We rope up, as the crevasses are deep and concealed by new snow. After 300m of walking straight down a 30° slope, I look at our prospective route and notice that the nose of the glacier we must descend to reach Magdalena Fjord rears up out of the water, without the piles of moraine we need to bridge our route to the shore. The glacier ends in a cliff. The fjord is inaccessible.

Tig and I bumble our way back up to the col. I am not sorry to miss the long, slippery walk along the Gullybreen glacier. We return over the thick bouncy bright green moss. A pair of skuas comes swooping across our path. As we continue to walk in the direction of their nest they begin their slow, injured dance, stamping on the ground, trailing a wing. Exhausted and with very wet feet we reach the shore, lie down and wait for the seals. They do not return, but the boys do. So in a light drizzle we weigh anchor and motor over the bar.

27 July, 1130, 79°43′N, 11°8′E: motor out past a petticoat of light ice that lines the mouth of the fjord. There are strong currents in the

shallow passage. It is decided that we should go and investigate a glacier at very close quarters. We slip quietly into Sladdbukta, a small fjord at 79°43′N, 11°8′E. A great avalanche of stone falls from one of the peaks, boulders bouncing off the scree and tumbling into the fjord. We heave to about 500m from the Sellstrombreen glacier. It is 80′ high, the layers of ice twisted and folded. A grubby line of silt marks each snow melt. I glimpse a thin piece of the glacier elegantly drop from the face of the cliff. A few seconds later the valley rumbles with the clatter and splash of its fall. The air is very cold, the sea a startlingly bright blue-green. Will and I row very carefully out in the tender, photographing and sighing at the sight of Sellstrombreen. It is delicate work; the seat has fallen out of the dinghy, so I am crouching in the bow, taking great care not to tip us into the freezing water.

1430: delighted to be back in the boat. We are now motoring north up Smeerenburgfjorden towards Norgallet. *Dolphin*'s library reveals interesting sailing facts, as read to the crew by the skipper. In early July 1856, Lord Dufferin left Bioynøya, 400 miles south of Svalbard, in search of an ice-free passage to the island. After spending four weeks skirting 'a continuous field of ice which lay 150 miles off the southern cost of Spitzbergen', open sea and land was sighted:

> There beyond, lay an open sea! Open not only to the Northward and Westward, but also to the Eastward! You can imagine my excitement. 'Turn the hands up, Mr Wyse!' ''Bout ship!' 'Down with the helm!' 'Helm a-lee!' Up comes the schooner's head to the wind, the sails flapping with the noise of thunder – blocks rattling against the deck, as if they wanted to blow their brains out – ropes dancing about in galvanised coils, like mad serpents – and everything to an inexperienced eye in inextricable confusion; till gradually she pays off on the other tack – the sails stiffen into deal-boards – the staysail sheet is let go – and heeling over on the opposite side, again

> she darts forward over the sea like an arrow from the bow . . . playing leapfrog over the heavy seas, and staggering under her canvas, as if giddy with the same joyful excitement which made my own heart thump so loudly. [Dufferin: 169]

2000: the sun is bright and lavishly warm. We spend considerable time fishing on the flat calm fjord. I catch a small cod but then lose the line.

2330 79°48′N, 11°50′E, Hamiltonbukta: a huge glacier with a vast cave in its icy cliffs, calving sporadically with the usual solemn roar. To the east of the bay, on tall cliffs lined with a bright mossy grass, is a guillemot colony. The squawk of the birds is like a constant auction, with sporadic guffaws of righteous alarm and applause. It is midnight. We are on deck, reading in the warm glow of the bright sun.

Tuesday 28 July 0700: Capps rows ashore to get water. Tig on polar bear watch. Within a few minutes Tig sees one ambling along the shore. Anxious that Capps might end up as breakfast, Tig wakes the rest of the crew and grabs a flare, which we persuade him not to ignite.

By now the bear has noticed Capps. He pauses, sniffs the air, cranes his neck forward and starts to amble towards the shoreline. Capps, oblivious of his admirer, crouches by the stream collecting water. Three reindeer grazing under the cliff clamber higher up the slope. Their movement catches the bear's attention. He saunters purposefully after them. Capps is off the morning menu.

0930: the sky is blue and clear, the sea calm as we manoeuvre our way out of the light ice floating in Hamiltonbukta. We motor towards Nordaustlandet for two and a half hours. Then there is a great stretch of flat, limpid water on which float great pieces of felled Siberian timber. The flat water marks the meeting point of two currents. We are moving into a new seascape. To the north the *frostrøyk* turns the horizon into a vertical grey-blue wall of water that appears to be looming over us, leaping up in great lava-lamp curls. Looking southwest, the angular profile of the mountains merges and distorts into great tower blocks, as if Brighton seafront had been built along the shore in the matter of a morning. I have to work hard to remember that what I see is not real. There is not the slightest chance of being able to recognise the cliff-line from the chart. I feel quite daunted and lost, sailing into a seascape I cannot understand.

Wednesday 29 July, Mossellaguna, 79°52′N, 17°28′E: woke to calm and cloud-free skies. On the tiller for three hours. A lone puffin swooped around the bow and flew in a giant circle. I am sure it winked at me. At midday a wind from the north blew up.

1700, 80°19′N, 17°18′E: the air is getting colder and colder. Then we hit a belt of fragmented pack ice. Capps went up the rig and guided Will past a miniature kingdom of ice, complete with inland lakes and hummocks, spits and islands. The ice crackles and chinks ominously – the sound of juniper burning? After two hours motoring we came to Sjuøyane, where we could not lay an anchor because the shore was blocked with fast ice. We motored on eastwards through dark blue water to a cove just south of the Sjuøyane, where we set the anchor. Will goes for a swim. Then he slowly puts on all the clothes he has brought with him. He is unusually quiet that evening.

30 July, 80°30′N, 19°55′E: within fifteen minutes of our retiring to our bunks, a wind blew up and hummed in the rigging and the anchor chain began to grind. Will noticed that the loose ice was beginning to float into the bay. We took up the anchor and motored to a new cove to the east side of Parryøya, where the anchor held fast. We are now 600 miles from the North Pole, and probably the most northerly sailing boat in the world.

I had hoped that the pack ice would be stunningly white against the majestic blue of the sky. But here the sea is flat and grey, and everything is grey and groans in the wind, and a mist lowers over us. It reminds me of the Bristol Channel on a dull day in February. I wonder how much of the world survives under this weather. We are at Parryøya on exactly the same date as Captain Parry's 1773 expedition in *Race Horse* and *Carcass,* with a crew that included the young Nelson. I am pleased to note that I am not the only one to have suffered Polar wooden boat dismay: the crew of the *Race Horse* found it 'a most desolate appearance indeed'.

31 July: on deck wearing two hats. It is still very cold. I fail to take up the invitation to walk on the island. I watch the boys row to the shore. Delighted to be on my own, I go downstairs for a little domestic bliss. I sweep the floor, put the pastry in the oven and am just going up the companionway to throw the dust over the stern when I see a clutch of terns swooping and diving around a polar bear. He swims towards *Dolphin,* nonchalant and calm, sniffing the air. Every now and then he pauses, as if he can smell the pastry cooking – or is it me? I am rather anxious.

I creep back down into the cabin, turn off the oven and quietly close the doors, wishing that the lock had been mended. The boys have taken the gun and all the flares. But then the bear seems so sophisticated and relaxed on what appears to be his morning constitutional, and I do not want to alarm him.

Peeping out through the ventilation holes, I can see that he is still swimming towards the boat. He stops and dips his head in the water, as if he is looking to calculate the depth of the hull. My heart is racing now. I watch him at very close quarters as he scrutinises the boat, then swims around it and heads for the shore. I wonder if he will bump into the rest of the crew.

He doesn't.

1 August, 1100: The northeasterly has finally dropped. Mist covers the island of Martensøya and Parryøya. We decide to move, and anchor in a bay on the west side of Phippsøya, about half a mile

from the shore. The sound of the water lapping at its edge reminds me of days spent moored up against other boats in various convivial marinas in Wales and Ireland. The world is still, grey and very cold. We go below decks. Luckily it is Saturday Night, Will's drinking night, so we have two glasses of rum each. Will beats Tig at chess. At about midnight we go to sleep. Twenty minutes later there is a loud grinding sound. I assume it is the anchor dragging on the rock. It sounds as if the fluke is not taking. The scraping noise continues. It becomes increasingly insistent and harsh. I peep out of the starboard porthole.

Dolphin is surrounded by flat ice. We pull on some clothes and scramble on deck to find a piece of flat ice the size of two rugby pitches bearing down on us. The anchor chain is already caught under the ice. While Capps, Will and I stand on the foredeck taking this in, *Dolphin*'s bow is being pulled downwards, as if she were about to dive under the ice. Capps turns on the engine and motors hard astern to see if we can pull the anchor out. We are firmly stuck. Next we try to ram the ice. It does not so much as crack. We are being pushed towards the shore. We have very little time before *Dolphin* will be crushed against the fast ice. Will and I pull out the entire hundred metres of chain. He ties two fenders to the bitter end, so that if we do have to slip the anchor we will have at least a chance of spotting it again.

Capps now suggests we try to manoeuvre *Dolphin* to the starboard edge of the floe, in the hope that pulled from the new angle the anchor will turn on its fluke and break out. We hastily agree. Capps edges the boat back and forth. On the fourth curve she roars forward, dragging the anchor with her. We stow it quickly. Within ten minutes the fenders are hanging back on their hook in the heads. Carefully we negotiate our way out into the loose pack ice.

We anchor on the east side of Martensøya in a bay that is clear of ice, although an impenetrable floe at the mouth of the bay is moving north at quite a rate. We agree to stand forty-five-minute watches to ensure that we do not get icebound again that night.

2 August, 80°39′N, 21°14′E: the following day we wend our way through a belt of 5/10 ice. We motor tentatively through the leads, guided by Will on the crosstrees. An eerie mist floats above the ice; the visibility at points is no more than ten yards. The ice has formed great modernist ridges and blocks. It is like wandering around a glamorous but empty housing development. We finally anchor on the eastern shore of Chermsideøya. Less than five days ago we were chased out of there by the predatory ice. It is now completely ice free.

But within eight hours we are moved on again by big pieces of ice that are floating on an apparently new current, straight into the bay. We heave up the anchor and motor east past cliffs of rose-pink granite, looking for somewhere to shelter. The water is astonishingly clear here. For the first time I notice sea shells on the sand and small, vigorously wiggling centipedes sauntering through the water.

We are not circumnavigating Svalbard; we are just mucking around in the ice. Each day we are caught out by the endless changes in the weather and ice conditions. We do not have the technology to analyse and predict patterns. We seem to have gone Polar barmy. We go to sleep at 1400 and wake at 1100. Every plan and intention is disrupted by the ice, which seems to be positively chasing us. All we are really doing is waiting for the ice to melt, watching the guillemots roost on steep cliffs and trying to avoid getting sunk. A few minutes' domestic bliss, cleaning and sweeping, proves energising. Raising the anchor and mainsail are also good for getting warm. I am beginning to wonder if we will ever get near the icepack, let alone sail any further east than Kapp Platen, the most northeasterly point of Nordaustlandet.

3 August, 80°31′N, 20°5′E. We row ashore and climb a fabulously rocky hill covered in great slabs of granite. Quite a scramble. From the top you can look east to Scoresbyøya and Oskarland, which is surrounded by ice. Right on the horizon under the ice-blink is the

pack ice, shimmering and white as far as the eye can see. There is no wind. It is quite still, totally silent, and warm, too, thanks to the brisk ascent. It is perfectly beautiful, empty and quite enormous. It feels fragile and utterly delicate; I know that within months the wind and the ice will be crashing and roaring across this vast, desolate seascape.

It is quite clear that there is no chance of our being able to circumnavigate the archipelago.

3 August, 1400, 80°31′N, 20°5′E, we motor over to the south end of Beverly Sundet. The sea is a brilliant blue. There is a light, brisk wind, so we sail east towards Scoresbyøya and Oskarland. The bay is completely uncharted. I stand on the bow and look out for shallows. With the sun on my face and the sound of the gently lapping water I imagine I am sailing in Greece – until I look up to see the huge icecap-smoothed mountains of the Nordaustlandet scarfed with vast white glaciers. We sail on until the fast ice of Scoresbyøya blocks our passage. We tack back. By 2100 the sky is mottled with mackerel clouds and the eastern hills have pulled on discreet veils and bonnets of grey mist.

We are just planning our supper and anchorage when down Beverly Sundet sail two gleaming plastic yachts with Norwegian flags. They are the first boats we have encountered for weeks, and they might have some spare vegetables and a weather update. We stand on deck and smile at five grey-haired men in matching blue wet weather gear. They stare sternly back at us. We sail gently past, and further on down to the Sound. Then over the radio we hear, in strong Norwegian tones: 'Is that Roger Capps? Tell me is that Roger Capps?'

It is Sverre Kræmer, a friend and veteran arctic explorer who was awarded the Tilman medal by the Royal Cruising Club for his arctic sailing. He had been below decks when we had passed each other. His crew reported that they had seen a wooden boat full of outlandishly dressed crew, obviously Russians. Having met us in Norway two years previously, he guessed it must be *Dolphin*.

We went about and anchored close by for a luxurious meal in their warm, fragrant boat. The crew were a group of Norwegian businessmen who had made their fortunes in Svalbard. Like us, they had hoped to circumnavigate Svalbard but they confirmed our suspicion that the ice would retreat no further. They had decided to give up and sail back to Longyearbyen. We would have to go south too.

After a number of hours of convivial conversation in the warm cabin, the *Dolphin*'s crew began to emit quite a distinctive smell of diesel, wool and effort. It was time to go. They gave us some radishes, biscuits and a detailed weather forecast. Next day they left early, tacking swiftly against a strong westerly. In less than an hour they were out of sight. They planned to be back in Longyearbyen within four days.

References:

Letters from High Latitudes, the Marquess of Dufferin, John Murray, eleventh edition, 1903

Den Norske Los: Arctic Pilot, Travellers' Club, 1990

Rank Amateurs

Fraser Fraser-Harris and John Clegg

When Commodore Vernon Nicholson began a yacht-chartering venture out of Nelson's dockyard in English Harbour, Antigua, sixty-three years ago, things were very different from the streamlined, organised, thoroughly professional charter trade of this year's winter season. In contrast to today's thousands of new and nearly new vessels, there were only a few boats, and most of them were veterans (as were many of their skippers). A series of articles published in *National Geographic* by Carleton Mitchell extolled the sailing virtues of the Windward and Leeward Islands, from Antigua south to Grenada, and caused northern yachtsmen to dream of trade winds, trackless beaches, exotic towns and roadsteads and islands in the sun. The Federation of the West Indies was tottering through its brief and uncertain existence, with crops of sugar, spices and bananas the main source of revenue on islands unchanged for a century. The bananas were loaded into ships belonging to Geest, a British fruiterer, by processions of energetic ladies who carried enormous stems aboard their heads and then ran back to the tallyman for another load. Canadian Pacific 'Lady Boats' took down cargoes of timber and salt fish and a smattering of tourist passengers to return laden with sugar and rum. (A bottle of the finest Mount Gay then cost less than a dollar 'Bee Wee' – British West Indian currency – about 50¢ US)

Not necessarily for this reason, but perhaps influenced by it, Lynton Rigg had moved down to Carriacou and opened the 'inn-famous' Mermaid Tavern with an ever-changing staff of glamorous Aer Lingus hostesses on holiday, along with the odd Canadian Colonel helping out with the distribution and consumption of its stock. Lynton's other contribution was the establishment of the Carriacou regatta for local workboats, a follow-on from the Out Island Regatta he had pioneered in the Bahamas. Later, yachts joined in, racing up from Grenada and down from Martinique in a forerunner of Antigua S Week.

Early Nicholson charter guests, nearly all members of Antigua's Mill Reef Club, founded by old American families with old American money, came down from Newport to enjoy the winter weather. The word soon spread around the cocktail circuits of New England and Canada, and demand for a larger fleet built up. These people wanted yachts with comfortable quarters, polished brass, varnished teak and good service from competent crews. Ever the entrepreneur, Commander Nicholson went back to Britain in search of suitable vessels, persuading their owners to sail out and join the fun.

To be financially viable, yachts had to be bought cheaply, so almost all were classic pre-war vessels with magnificent old slow-turning engines for which spare parts were nowhere available. Their electrics were primitive and minimal, of strange voltages, and with junction boxes full of electrocuted cockroaches. The lead-covered cable often carried as many volts in the insulation as there were in the batteries. Most boats had plough-steel rigging, wormed, parcelled and served, tensioned by galvanised bottlescrews packed in white lead and tallow, sewn in canvas and painted. Some even had lignum vitae deadeyes with four-stranded Italian tarred hemp lanyards started with a double Matthew Walker and finished with a cow hitch, the tail slipped back on itself with frapping turns to make all secure. One did not tune the rigging very often!

Canvas sails needed frequent washing and drying to hold their shape and defy mildew. Manila cordage shrank when wet and relaxed when dry, requiring endless tending of throat and peak halyards, topsail tack downhauls and dinghy lashings. It was good old-fashioned stuff, and we who were privileged to sail and keep these vessels took it seriously. We stitched sails by hand and roped them ourselves. The island sugar factories were invited from time to time to make bits and pieces on the huge lathes in their workshops, which normally turned nothing weighing less than a ton. Perforce we used our ingenuity. Once the commander ran a whole charter in the 135′ schooner *Te Vega* without a starter motor. A 1/2″ line was led four times around the enormous flywheel of the Glennifer, up through the engine room skylight to a snatch block on the boom and thence forward. At a cry from below, the entire crew, mustered on the hauling part, rushed forward. On the third revolution the commander dropped the exhaust valve lifts and the two-ton complex of iron, steel and rust burst into song like a seagull.

By 1959, when John Clegg first arrived in English Harbour skippering the French tunnyman *Georgiana* for Mike Willoughby, who was then running *Te Vega* (a topsail schooner which ran aground if she moved in English Harbour at the bottom of the tide), he was greeted by the commander as the twelfth sailing vessel to join the fleet. Those already present were such old favourites as *Mollyhawk*, the pretty little schooner in which the Nicholson family had originally set off from Ireland bound for New Zealand, kept perfectly by Jol Byerley and his beautiful wife Jenny; *Voyageur* and *Lady Phyllis*, two magnificent 115′ Herreshoff schooners owned by Walter Boudreau from Nova Scotia; *Pas de Loup*, another yacht conversion of a tunnyman; *Maverick*, a Brixham trawler built of teak as a yacht in the 1930s; *Harebell*, a handsome 70′ steel ketch by Rasmussen; *Tern III*; *Aurora*; *Te Vega*; *Dayspring*, another converted fisherman and senior vessel in the port by virtue of her White Ensign (skippered by ex-Royal Navy Captain Bruno Brown); and *Zambesi* run by Ian Spencer. *Zambesi* stood out as the only Bermuda rig in the fleet. *Xebec*, the lone powerboat, was a very graceful old steam yacht converted to diesel.

If the commander influenced the selection of boats, his daughter-in-law Julie made it quite clear how they were to be run. She handled all the correspondence with potential charterers, and her golden opinion was worth having. Her ideas were sound and directed at sending charter guests home happy. Indeed, this was the goal for us all, and those who succeeded were rewarded with more charters. Some of her notions owed a lot to her Maine girlhood. She was convinced that every skipper should be married to his beloved (too much Henry Miller under the Blue Hill bedclothes by flashlight), and that a bidet was only useful for 'wicked washing' and had no place in a respectable charter yacht. Like Nelson, in whose footsteps she followed around the dockyard, she could turn a blind eye. Her powers of imagination became legend. Such phrases as 'dine in the cockpit by candlelight' creating the illusion of tropical romance at its best, could often be factually interpreted as 'candles are the only source of illumination on board, and after a meal has been cooked the saloon is uninhabitable.' She was known affectionately as Alice in Wonderland for her literary prowess, but none could challenge its effectiveness. One of her favourites among us was later to be respected by some and envied by most for contriving to sell two successful yachts to an insurance company for considerably more than their market value. His guests, peering backwards through an alcoholic haze which all but obscured the memory of their cruise, missed the squalor and chaos, the burnt-out galley and the dinghy on the stern davits often filled with inadvertently-flung garbage. They remembered only the joy of the sailing, the bonhomie of the company, and the wild Bacchantic nobility of their skipper.

The *Xebec* brochure was as beautiful as the old motor yacht herself seen from a distance. It did not, however, mention the two large dogs kept by the captain on the boat deck. They frequently lifted a leg to a stanchion, and the guests below on the fantail doubtless felt that even the islands' rain was tinged with sunshine.

Skippers and crews were a mixed bag: ex-British submarine commanders and other ex-Navy and Merchant-Navy types along with keen amateur yachtsmen who had escaped the austerity of post-war Britain. Later, German, French, Canadian and American young men and women came 'down island' to join the fleet, abandoning civilisation in search of both wealth (not likely) and good health (plenty of it).

The Admiral's Inn in Nelson's Dockyard was another Nicholson family project. It was here in 1964 that Don Street and your co-author, Fraser Fraser-Harris first met. I had come down from Canada with the intention of buying *Mollyhawk* on the suggestion of my old friend Bruno Brown, skipper of *Freelance*. *Mollyhawk* turned out to be in poor shape by then, so I did not buy her. This did little to endear me to either the Nicholson family or the close-knit group of British skippers and their wives. Don, who had sailed his famous *Iolaire* down from the Virgins, felt the same cold draught upon his shoulder. One day, sitting in the Inn, he remarked that he had found a fine way to keep his beer cool. 'I buy it by the case,' he said, 'bring it in here, put it between my knees and announce that I have come to join the charter fleet. The atmosphere gets so God-damned cold that the beer freezes.' At about this time John Clegg reappeared from a sojourn in England with *Flica II*, a 12-meter which the Mashford yard had converted for him into a four-berth charter boat. She was changed to a ketch rig for this exotic cruising service.

My popularity with the other skippers did not improve when I became master of *Ring Anderson*, a 95′ Baltic Trader owned and expensively converted to a luxury charter yacht by a fellow Canadian, Denis Love. As a just-retired Canadian Navy Commodore, no doubt my late broad stripe was still showing. Nor was I aware that the job had already been more or less promised to a popular local. *Ring*, built in the Ring Anderson yard in Denmark in 1945, with her old-world charm and modern comfort, vied then with *Panda* as Queen of the Fleet. And it was not too long before I, too, relishing the novel joy of turning a hobby into a profession, became as piratical as any member of the Antigua chartering establishment, a group proud to call itself the 'Seagoing Pub-keepers Union.' I recall reacting in much the same way, about a year later, to another newcomer, a very British ex-army, ex-Kenya senior policeman. Announcing his name as Sam Browne, he added, 'You won't forget the name. My grandfather invented the belt.' The same evening, at a cocktail party aboard *Ring,* I could not resist introducing him as Mr Jock Strap. The name stuck, but despite this we became good friends.

When I left the islands some years later, John and Sally Clegg took over *Ring Andersen*. There could scarcely have been a greater contrast than between *Flica II,* John's former command, and *Ring* – *Flica II* described by Johnny Caldwell of *Outward Bound* as 'the bloody submarine' for her inclination to dive straight through waves, while *Ring* sailed over them with little speed but great dignity. Johnny Caldwell, intent on replanting the beaches with royal palms, was famous for hoarding water for his infant trees and keeping his guests short.

As well as the labour required to maintain your vessel in serviceable condition without assistance from a real boatyard, there was the domestic chore of providing first-class meals with only the very primitive shopping facilities of the various islands. In Antigua, on a Saturday, meat was bought in the village of All Saints. If you arrived too early, the steak was liable to be still tethered to a stake, lowing. You bought meat 'with bone' or meat 'without bone'. T-bone steaks came at the lower price. 'Stand outside, Skip, or your shirt get nasty', the butcher would say cheerfully, as he laid into a carcass with machete and saw, swatting flies and moving interested dogs with the flat of his cutlass.

Antigua did at least have a 'supermarket' in St Johns, but in St Lucia you queued up to recite your needs to an unbelieving young lady who would fetch each item, tin by tin, from the shelves, writing it all down on the bill in longhand. By the time enough food, drink, cosmetics, soap and toilet paper for twelve people for a fortnight had been gathered, everyone concerned, including the other customers, was hot, tired and bad-tempered.

Each charter lasted ten to fourteen days. Our guests ranged from young and enthusiastic doctors from Montreal or Toronto reliving their student days, to sedate New Englanders or wealthy Torontonians who intended to enjoy good service and ideal cruising conditions. A good skipper had to be both psychologist and chameleon, adjusting to the character and mood of the guests, keeping them amused, soothed, enlightened and happy. *Ring* was fortunate in her West Indian crew; not only were they fine seamen and good shipmates, but they were also delighted to form their own band. Since there was little organised diversion ashore, skippers and/or their mates often had to conduct guided tours and expound upon the history and special features of individual islands. Beach and snorkel parties required unobtrusive supervision and instruction on the natural hazards of West Indian beaches, which range from sunstroke to manchineel or beach apples, this last an inviting fruit resembling a tangerine. It is not to be tasted, ever. Even touching it can burn the skin; swallowing the juice can be fatal.

Running a charter boat was no holiday afloat. During voyages our days began early. The deck had to be cleaned, scrubbed and polished before breakfast. Guests would swim over the side or be taken ashore to nearby beaches. In the forenoons, after breakfast, a passage was made between anchorages, with lunch served along the way. Then it was down anchor and out boats and off on expeditions. Back aboard for cocktails at sunset, in the welcome cool of the evening captain and mate became host and hostess with questions to answer on activities and stories to be exchanged. Dinner was a highlight of each day and competition was keen among cooks set on establishing a cordon-bleu reputation – no small task on a tiny stove with limited supplies, but essential to a successful charter season.

A popular alternative was the beach barbecue on white powder sands beneath a floodlit moon and bright tropical stars to music from the ship's company or the skipper's guitar, the whole lubricated with ice-cold rum punches made from good rum and fresh limes, borne ashore in Thermos flasks. Not surprisingly, many a nymph enjoyed a chase into the warm phosphorescent water pursued by an enthusiastic satyr. By the time order was restored, and the guests escorted back aboard to tumble into their bunks, the next day was already dawning.

Most skippers had their favourite taxi drivers on each island. Selected both for the reliability of their sometimes ancient vehicles, and for their friendly personalities, these men would wait for the arrival of their yachts. They could be trusted not only to give guests a good time, show them interesting things and bring them safely back, but also to provide welcome extras in the galley. They could supply delicacies like freshwater prawns from the mountain rivers, fish from the local fishermen, bananas, pineapples and fresh local vegetables from their friends.

Particular islands offered particular entertainments. In Dominica, where there was a suitable anchorage at each end of the sombre, mountainous island, an enterprising young Englishman ran a 'safari' service. Land Rovers driven by good-looking islanders dressed in white robes and a red fez, the traditional garb of a Kenya guide, collected the guests. They were first taken up into the rainforest to spectacular clear pools under shimmering waterfalls where they could swim, if they felt so inclined, in the unusually cold water. Then the safari would proceed to a plateau overlooking the Atlantic, where picnic tables were rigged, complete with white linen cloths and silver service. Some refreshing glasses of champagne preceded a veritable banquet, after which, duly rested and somewhat bemused by such unexpected luxury, they were driven back down the mountain to rendezvous with the yacht, which had travelled up or down the island as they frolicked.

Shortly before leaving the Caribbean, I heard that this enterprising young man had requested permission to add a family of elephants to the local fauna, which already included monkeys and parrots. The politicians, I think wisely, anticipated that on this small island they might find themselves up to their armpits in elephants. The permit was refused.

Completely different, but equally enjoyed by all, was the hospitality offered in Bequia by Sidney MacIntosh, descendant of one of the early Scottish settlers, and his American wife Enid from Baltimore. They lived in an old stone cottage, kept chickens and had a fine vegetable garden. Two or three times a week during the charter season they laid on barbecue parties for yacht guests, sometimes for two or three groups at the same time. Enid and her daughter produced mammoth spreads of delicious local foods while Sidney served and partook of generous measures of rum punch. Supported by an island band that he had taught to play highland reels in addition to the island repertoire, he created an atmosphere of sheer fun which few could resist. Exhausted but happy, the guests would be loaded into Land Rovers of uncertain vintage, driven back to the harbour and poured into the boats. Early the next morning Sidney would appear on the jetty with fresh vegetables and eggs for the ship's larder, looking as though he had slept the night through.

Arrangements for such excursions were made in advance on the Children's Hour, the commander's daily broadcast from English Harbour. Important messages to and from yachts cruising down-island were also passed by this means. There was of course no security attached to these exchanges, and they gave considerable entertainment to all concerned. One unhappy charterer received a telegram which read, 'Come home. All is forgiven.' The air immediately filled with much ribald and anonymous advice: 'Go home, you bum.' 'It's a trap, don't touch it.' 'Stay here and have fun.'

Entertainment was only part of our function in life. More serious and equally important were good sailing and safe passages. Yachts seldom took trips at night, as both crew and passengers became too tired. Exceptions were, however, made when full-moon conditions were so delightful that the experience was irresistible. Literally steering by the stars in calm seas and the light breezes of the night, with the shadow of the islands on the horizon, was unforgettable. Occasionally a school of dolphin would investigate the vessel, their blowing in the dark resembling the heavy breathing of a herd of cattle in a field.

Reefs were unmarked and the coasts unlit except for the odd lighthouse; so safe navigation required the same detailed local knowledge as the choice of interesting and comfortable anchorages. Don Street was only then doing the groundwork for the guidebooks and charts of West Indian waters which subsequently brought him a different fame.

From November through March and into April, the Trade Winds blow steadily out of a direction north of east, reaching their maximum velocity during December, when they are known locally as the Christmas winds. At this time they may exceed 15 knots, gusting 20 for days on end. Since the channels between the islands are open to the Atlantic, there can be a fair buildup of sea – particularly in the long passage between Antigua and Guadeloupe. Novice charter guests coming suddenly into this seaway, in which adjacent yachts might disappear from view, sometimes found the experience frightening. For those of us working the vessels, these passages – close-hauled coming up-island, reaching when southbound – were often exhilarating and sometimes exhausting, but rarely tricky unless there were numerous black or white squalls. These demanded avoiding action if possible, and reduced canvas if not. The quiet waters to leeward of an island provided a welcome relief, particularly for the bad sailors.

If passengers were to enjoy these adventures to the full, crews had to instil confidence. In *Ring* we began each charter with a forenoon briefing accompanied by a welcoming bottle or two of champagne. Assembled aft on the fantail, the forthcoming trip was discussed, detailed plans were made according to the guests' preferences in respect of particular islands and anchorages to be visited, and various tips and warnings given. Among these, sunburn, the worst enemy of the northern winter visitor, had priority. Suggestions that cotton clothing should be worn in preference to synthetics, which can cause uncomfortable rashes in hot weather, might have seemed self-evident. Ventilation was another point covered. Yachts of dark colour and heavy timbers such as *Ring* retained a lot of heat at the end of the day and good ventilation through the vessel was essential to comfortable sleep. One such briefing was interrupted by the glamorous wife of a guest, who said, 'What goes on here, Skipper? First you take my nightie off, and now you've got my cabin door open.'

In 1966, Denis Love bought Grenada Yacht Services and *Ring* moved south to base there. Thus began the buildup of a second charter fleet in competition with the Nicholsons. Grenada Yacht Services was designed for its support. The late 60s saw a rapid expansion of both fleets, and change in the character of the yachts. Modern fibreglass vessels replaced the veterans. Ashore, considerable development was beginning, some of it undertaken by yacht owners, their skippers and guests.

At about this time, bareboats also made their debut down-island. This was an innovation not welcomed by the old pros in the manned fleets. It destroyed our monopoly, and it created problems hitherto unknown. Since the bareboats were often chartered by enthusiastic amateurs whose inexperience was matched by their ignorance of local waters, they frequently had to be rescued from embarrassing situations. In those early days they lacked the support which now sends them out well-instructed, pre-provisioned and attended by chase boats ready to come to their aid.

Progress was also accompanied by politics. Island authorities began to see the charter boats as a source of revenue, and gradually subjected them to unwelcome bureaucratic attention. And as aircraft and cruise liners brought yet more tourists in quantity, hotels multiplied, everything became busier and more demanding, and local people became restless as their peaceful territories were invaded by the wealthy. Cultures clashed. Gradually, the sense of splendid isolation from the world outside began to fade. When the British turned over the island of Grenada to the stewardship of a mountebank whom the people did not trust, and compounded this irresponsible act by awarding him a knighthood, it seemed time to leave Nirvana and return to wearing shoes, long pants, collars and ties. And so Fraser-Harris, retired Canadian Navy Commodore and subsequently West Indian charter skipper, did.

But that six-year interlude between the disciplined lifetime of a combat service in war and peace and a return to civilian employment remains a precious memory. It was, for so many of us, the time when we amateur sailors became professionals. The Adnan Khashoggis, Donald Trumps and others of the macrobuck brigade have obtained their expert yacht skippers from this school.

As well as our professionalism, we are left with recollections of early morning in a totally still anchorage, the edge of the water motionless upon the sand. And later in the day, under water, feeding jewelfish from a broken sea urchin held on the blade of a knife, sunlight shimmering from the bright corals below. And sunsets, muscles tired from hours spent behind the wheel in a seaway, watching for the green flash. These were the riches we shared with our charter guests. It is not surprising that many of them became lifelong friends.

Childhood Sailing in the Fifties

John Simpson

Dauntless, our family's first boat, was a 12-ton Lowestoft fishing smack of uncertain vintage. It took my father three years of his spare time to convert her into a pleasure yacht, working on her in a mud berth on the salting at Brandy Hole on the upper reaches of the River Crouch in Essex.

Given my parents' personal circumstances – two young kids and living in a rented flat – this was an optimistic decision; but they were both only thirty at the time, and having survived the war they wanted some quality of life. My father was a clever man, and very good with his hands. He needed to be, as the smack had little accommodation except her original fish holds. He converted these into three cabins, galley and head, and gave them light and headroom by building two coachhouses on the flush decks.

His main difficultly was fitting the bearers for the engine, which came out of a car abandoned on the marsh. The oak frames were so well pickled with salt water that it was almost impossible to drill into them. A six-inch nail given a good clout with a lump hammer would make no impression, and drill bits snapped off like pencil leads. He finally finished all the work by 1951, and we started sailing the boat as a family.

None of the enormous amount of work my parents put into the boat meant much to me at the time, as my sister and I were playing on the marshes or up to some other mischief. (Our great family friend Len Warren remembers us finding his carefully collected hoard of oysters, stored in the mud under one of the dinghy slips, and selling them to the local restaurant for money to buy sweets. He wasn't too happy.)

Most weekends we sailed as a family of four, but for the annual two-week summer holiday my mother's sister Vera and her family teamed up with us.

Our early joint family summer cruises were at first limited to the east coast rivers. Len Warren joined us, providing expertise and strength to cope with the smack's heavy gear. He was totally unflappable, having flown a record number of bombing missions as an RAF navigator.

By 1955, when I was seven, *Dauntless* and her crew of nine were ready to go foreign for the first time. This is Len's log of the cruise:

> **Sun 20 Aug.** 0515. Reveille, thick mist, no wind, so engine down river slowly with tide & anchor at W Buxey until tide turns. Alfresco dinner & siesta until 1400 then beat against tide & NE – rough & leaking badly. Reach Swin Spitway by 1800 – wind falling, sickness aboard so sail into calm water & anchor near Clacton. Keep anchor watch; but very calm.
>
> **Mon.** Make & mend & wash down on deck, then all ashore (five adults & four kids) for sunbathing & supplies & swimming & collecting shells. (Yobos board boat while we're ashore, but nothing stolen.) Set sail at 1600 with tide against us & NE wind. Fairly short boards, 1920 Walton, becoming dark but weather settled so scrap idea of Walton Backwaters & head out for Sunk Light. 2210 sight sunk pilot boat, engine across busy shipping lane & head for Long Sand Head buoy. Wind dying down.
>
> **Tues.** 0015. Engine at full bore for 45mins to stem tide round buoy, then c/c SE, 3 knots. Ken sleeps while Jim &

I keep watch. Dawn breaks & thick mist, sirens all round. Spend all morning having catnaps, dinner in sunshine. 1600 hear W Hinder to starboard (15 miles?), 2000 pass Ostend pilot. Surrounded by wreck buoys. Sight Ostend light & beat up coast in darkness pursued by shipping. Flash torch at them & are inspected by searchlight. Finally cross shipping lane & anchor 2 1/2 miles from Blankenburgh, about a mile off-shore, while tide floods strongly. Anchor watch & inspected by mysterious motor boat, anchor warp is well stretched. Plenty of phosphorescence.

Set sail at 0530. **Wed** & beat up coast in thick mist & NW wind past Zeebrugge. Wake up to find us surrounded by shipping so motor inshore – tide carries us back to Blankenburgh pier. Anchor for pumping (leaking stern glands) & dinner. Wind freshens so use engine to clear a lee shore, rough & rolling. At 1500 we re-pass wreck that we passed at 0600. Wind backs & we hold e'ly course past Zeebrugge. In irons on tack so gybe her round & out N. Heavy seas knock down speed so down mainsail & run into Zeebrugge under headsails & engine. Turn into Yacht haven & lay alongside pontoon. Quite an arrival – me in holey socks, Jim's seat out of trousers, Ken's pom-pom hat & a coil of new rope (hemp?) all snarled up. Ashore for three beers in café (very strong at 7p a glass). Back, supper & clean up of boat. Bad leak in prop gland. Chat with Belgian businessman. 130frs to £1.

Thurs. Spend morning sampling beer, arranging to slip boat at local café & looking at shops. Then steak & chips (40frs) at café. Send home postcards. Cigarettes 8/11 for 25. Afternoon looking at train times & concert party on beach. Padre tips cap at me! (Halo showing.)

Fri. Women & kids off to Bruges. Engine across harbour, past fishing fleet, fish market, artists, withy pontoon (for sea defences) & onto slipway by 2030. Lay up against last pile – everyone advises us it's dangerous but cast around with lead & decide to chance it. Heavy rain while tide ebbs away but soon repack gland from dinghy. Buy smock (95frs) & then beer, eggs & bacon for dinner & wait for tide. Tread on Jim's fingers while descending ladder. Finish money on cigarettes. Fishing boats stream in & delay our departure back to pontoon.

Sat. Up at 0500 & motor out with tide s wind, calm. Set sails & make 4 knots. 0800 cross Belgian frontier, signalled by a Bristol ship. Follow coast round & into Breskens harbour – mixed up with ferry. Tight turns in harbour with bowsprit missing everything by inches. Tie up & ashore for beer & supplies – cheese, new bread. 10 guilders to £1. 1500 catch free ferry to Flushing & inspect canal & send postcard. Buy sheath knife & egg slice, eggs etc. Chat with Dutch over one side & Belgian the other. 2100 walk round town with Jim & Peggy, listen to military band & so to bed.

Sun. Ashore for petrol & ash-tray souvenirs. Then warp out & motor though harbour. Set headsails, over to Flushing. 5 MVs, 2 ferries & 2 yachts all converging at one point but sorts itself out. Go straight through lock. Tie up at 1st bridge (shut till 1900). Good lunch on board. Visited by customs & passports stamped. Clear eel from lavatory, a messy business, with eel stuck up inlet pipe, and decapitated by gate-valve. Bridge opens at 1930 so through into canal. 2100 run ashore at Middleburgh & knock up bridge-keeper (bridge closed). He opens up & we motor slowly into a dark basin & moor off swimming pool with boat-hook holding stern in deep end. Explore canals & bridges in dark, sample beer & send postcard.

Mon. Awake by 0600 to check boathook & depth (9″ under keel). All ashore while I remain aboard & check route home. 1400 motor along to Vere & tie up by spare lock gates – chat with Flushing Yacht Club members (promise to send burgee to them). Inspect locks (pile-driver blocking entrance) lend chart to yacht from Sandwich to Cologne. Watch fishermen landing catch in fishing harbour. Supplies of water & petrol & finish up in beer cellar.

Tues. Wash down, booked out by Customs. 1030 follow

barge through lock & tie up for final supplies and wait for tide. 1345 set course & motor down Vere Gat NW wind. 1500 entrance of Vere Gat. Set sail on NW course. 1900 reach last buoy & becalmed for rest of night in sight of W Capelle & wreck buoy. Drift up and down with tide & round in circles. Flash fishing boat that approaches too near.

Wed. 0700. Very light W wind, tide carrying us north. 1400 hear Galloper siren (25-30 miles) can't see N Hinder. Wind swings SW so set w'ly course for Galloper, very calm.

Thurs. 0200. Strong NW pipes up so sail SW on other tack. Boil along at 5 1/2 knots & sight Galloper (DR 3 miles out). 1600 Galloper c/c Kentish Knock. 0630 Kentish Knock c/c Tongue – roughly 0900 Tongue light, engine on to creep past Margate sands, on to Herne Bay then turn NW as wind backs to W to pass E Spaniard, Barrow 17 & W Swin – very heavy & close, slight rain. Follow buoys up Swin to Whittaker (1700). Engine against strong SW (I sleep like a log for 3hrs) anchor at Shore – ends at 2200 after steering reciprocals of back – bearings, from S Buxey.

Fri. 1000. Strong SW wind. Anchor drags so motor into Roach & lay to anchor & kedge. Ashore to Churchend for supplies & phone Customs & Brandy Hole. Visited by Customs & booked in 1900. Motor up with tide thro' Burnham (2100). Dark with rain. Touch bottom at Brandy Hole & she gets herself off. Pick up mooring at 2300 after 350 miles.

Fine weather & good luck offset headwinds.

We four children all slept in the forepeak, which Dad had converted into two berths with pipe cots above. My cousin Richard (six years older) decided he preferred the berths. His sister Lynne and my sister (both three years older) used to argue about the other berth. As the youngest I wasn't given a choice; I was always up in a pipe cot, which tended to come down in the night and land on the person below if you wriggled hard enough.

There were some memorable moments. Len would keep us amused in the cockpit in the evenings before bed, playing the mouth organ. Our big thrill was the midnight feasts supplied by the grownups – sweets (particularly imitation cigarettes), although once we were abroad, French fries became our favourite. The Harbour master at Flushing in Holland had a big plastic nose held on by elastic. Being a cheeky little boy, I asked what was wrong with his nose. To my horror he took it off and showed me. He had been a member of the Dutch resistance, and it had been burnt off by the Gestapo during torture.

We did the last joint family cruise on the *Dauntless* without Len Warren, who now had his own boat. Once again we crossed the North Sea to Holland. On the way home we were caught out in a nasty gale. The old girl sprung a bow plank, the mainsail ripped in half, and we used flares to signal that we were in distress. Assistance was rendered by a small Dutch coaster. The women and children were taken off – I can remember Dad waking us up and carrying me through the smack with water over the floorboards, and the Dutch captain's wife giving us toast, and my embarrassment at being carried along the dockside by a policeman, still in my pyjamas. *Dauntless* was towed into Lowestoft with my uncle and father still on board, pumping to keep her afloat. Our rescue made the national press.

Not surprisingly, my Uncle Kenneth decided to call it a day, and his family didn't come with us again.

Downriver with the Lightermen

Bob Harris

Thames lighters could carry fifty tons of cargo. They were propelled either by two oars near the bow, or a single oar over the stern. The oars were some twenty-five feet long.

Nine Elms to the Tower

I had worked up with a singlehanded barge on the flood tide to our wharf, receiving orders there from the foreman to take the *Jubilee* to the Royal Albert Dock, a new boy as mate. Spring tides were running, high water in the afternoon. This was about five to six hours' journey.

We started away from the wharf with the wind about south. My mate was very green. I was busily engaged in looking after him as the oar was unmanageable in his hands, I taking the pair with him hanging on to instruct him in the rhythm of swinging out and pulling steadily; he was really more trouble to me than the barge. I was sorry for him, as he had rowed up with the skiff and blisters were now forming on both hands. We allowed her to blow over to leeward, I explained that usually we had to row across the river to the Pimlico shore to get in a favourable working position to shoot Vauxhall. As the river bends towards Vauxhall the wind leads from aft, and it was a fair wind to Waterloo on this day.

An elderly, be-whiskered hoveller is rowing his boat near us. Hoveller is the term applied to a waterman who acts as a bridge pilot to sailing barges up through the bridges. This one was Tom Cunis, brother to Mr R Cunis the Master Lighterman. On reaching their destination they would assist in heaving up the mast and, on the return trip down along, would help raise it again at the mud-hole just above London Dock, Shadwell.

'Hello my old Banksider, and how are you, old man?' is the first greeting from him; he always prefixes with 'old man'. By this time he has come right alongside and having placed the sculls inboard is standing up in the boat, or dish as he calls her, and leans both arms on our gunwale. 'Where are you going old man?'

'Down the Albert,' replied I, in the vernacular.

We are now on the north side opposite Nine Elms Pier. I spot a friend at the coal wharf adjacent. Giving a long whistle, an imitation of a starling, I draw his attention. Up shoots his arm and then a shout. I am not certain of the words but sense that it is, 'Where are you going?' I wave down the river two from the elbow and one long one from the shoulder; he then knows that I am bound to somewhere in the lower reaches. This is a Friday and the gang always meet in the gallery at Gattis music hall. I raise my arms above my head waving them crosswise, scissor fashion; he now knows that this present job will prevent an appearance in the gallery tonight.

The tide is now beginning to run faster, and drawing the lad's attention to the nine arches of Vauxhall I point out the need to 'hold em up' to the north buttress of whichever arch you mean to work through. I take the oar aft for him and instruct him that when I say 'pull' to pull steadily and watch me. When I say 'give it to her' I mean pull as hard as you can. When you get the order 'the other way', reverse the oar at the stern post. There is now no time for talking, but our navigation is well in hand as we shoot No. 3 from the north'ard. Just below is the temporary bridge, but this is easy now as the middle arch is fairly wide.

As we pass the Tate Gallery, drawing the lad's attention to the figure of Britannia, I ask him what is wrong with the figure? The answer is that Britannia is holding the Trident in the right hand, whereas on the penny it is shown the reverse way; which is correct is a matter for dispute. Just below here a boat comes alongside our port side, a mop is shown over the stern to signify a buyer of old rope. His behaviour is somewhat unusual, standing up and peeping furtively down the river, and we follow his glance and notice on the Lambeth shore the River Police rowing up over the tide. As his boat is on the blind side to anyone on the south shore, he can see by peeping over the gunwale and remain unseen from the south bank. When out of the angle of vision he rows away chanting 'Old rope!' Possibly his transactions today have been without reproach, but he believes in safety first.

We are now at Lambeth Bridge, three arches only, my mate is getting his sea legs but not his river hands. I tell him not to look at them so often and he will forget them. The tide is by now full ebb and with a fresh breeze aft we are making good way: Lambeth Palace and later St Thomas's Hospital on the south bank, the Houses of Parliament and Big Ben on the north.

We are nearing Westminster Bridge and both of us are aft keeping her straight, as the tendency is for craft to come broadside to a wind. There is good way on her so pointing her to the centre of No. 4 arch we take the middle. A bundle of straw is hanging suspended in the centre of the arch. I explain this is a signal that repairs are being done at this spot to the bridge. When under the arch I gaze up into the staging; there is a painter pausing in his work looking down at our barge shooting through. Cupping both hands I yell so that the echoes ring (most bridges will produce an echo): 'What stinks worse than a painter?' A reply was expected, but not the reply, 'A dirty little barge boy!' He won. Here was I, in charge, with a new apprentice, patent to all observers, being actually considered by another workman a dirty little boy. I suffered from an inferiority complex for the next five minutes.

To regain my spirits I demonstrate to the lad how an oar should be handled. He is shown how to carry this from end to end of the craft, blade in water, speedily and safely, and how to throw it 'for'ard' for steering. It is essential for this to be smartly and correctly accomplished. An oar can easily take charge of its owner, especially when the craft has good headway going through the water, such as when entering slack water from the tideway, similar in fact to a novice in a row boat 'catching a crab'. The 'feel' of how to handle an oar, in this case twenty-eight-foot long, comes by practice. A real smart operation is to shift the oar from the rowing tack or crutch to the opposite side in one movement around the bow. This is done by walking smartly 'forward' with the oar, blade tilted, causing the blade to be parallel with the handle, then placing the point of balance on the bitt head or fore post, weighing down on the handle, and with a semi-circular movement – hands, arms and feet working in unison – the oar is flung say from port side to starboard. This may appear a lot of words, but I can assure anyone who may be interested in river work that these essentials formed an important item of 'under oar' work.

Our barge has begun to drift sideways during the lesson. We straighten her up just above Hungerford Bridge (Charing Cross). A sailing barge, mast on deck, sprit overhanging aft, mizzen set and drawing well, one man rowing, the skipper at the wheel, but no bridge sail or small lug set, quickly passes us. We notice 'Maldon' painted on the stern. There is not a hoveller in charge. This is rather unusual with an 'Essexman', their mode of procedure when without this pilot is to drop down with the tide, anchor dragging: this is termed 'gilling'.

The wind will shorten in the next reach. I have already decided to work No. 4 arch of Waterloo Bridge to be up to windward for the long stretch to Blackfriars. The set of tide at Waterloo is hard to north at all times of the ebb. We are now about halfway between Hungerford and Waterloo, mate aft, I for'ard edging her up to the south buttress of No. 4. The sailing barge, just below us, is in an excellent position to take this arch when suddenly he drops anchor 'all standing'. The effect caused by this action was that the 'sailorman' suddenly swung round head upon tide, the mate paying away fathoms of cable hand over hand, the barge sheering about as though resentful of this treatment. We were in a direct line astern: the skipper at the helm was steadying the sheering endeavouring to avoid us, while we were shaping to avoid him. The result was a glancing blow along our starboard side, no damage to either, but we are transformed from a live ship into a drifting hulk. The blow had caused my mate to lose his oar, our barge to lose her headway and drift sideways, me to lose my temper but (luckily for our governor) not my nut. We are almost at the bridge and though apparently in line for the arch I realise that with no headway, No. 4 was a doubtful starter. This is all in the space of minutes and now is the time to decide, and when decided, act.

Throwing the oar over to starboard I row hard to shape for No. 3 arch, then reversing our only oar to the port side we row about a dozen hard ones to straighten up. My decision was if we have got to hit the bridge we will do so on the 'soft' side, as it is termed, this meaning the tide is setting from that side, as opposed to the 'hard' side with the tide setting on. With the wind now 'short' we are helped into No. 3 arch just clear of touching. A spectator from the bridge would have anticipated a 'side-winder'.

There are now two things to do. Firstly, abuse the skipper of the sailorman, who had by now hove up short, dropping gently down above the bridge. He is told exactly in what part of the body I would have the pleasure of seeing him wearing that anchor. Secondly, recover the lost oar. When that was done our barge was on a lee shore near the Embankment. Several tugs passed under our head giving us their flop flop wash, which did not help matters, but we managed to row her out into the middle arch of Blackfriars.

In justice to sailormen, as sailing barge people are called by lightermen, they are a fine type of river and coastal men. The incident just related is local, the skipper – probably owner or part-owner – decided to save the hoveller's fee, but when confronted with the numerous arches of Waterloo, was not sure of himself – safety first.

By now I am quite happy again. As we pass my birthplace I give the Bankside whistle. Uncle Alf waves. Several labourers at the old iron wharf wave also. St Paul's is opposite.

The tide between Southwark and London Bridge runs, in my opinion, the fastest on the journey. There are several races of tide such as off Rosherville, Gravesend, but this rather narrow straight shoot of tide is always like a mill race. At this time of ebb tide there is a tidal set to the south at the middle of London Bridge, but at or from half ebb to low water the direction changes from a straight shoot through to one hard to the north buttress.

The river below London Bridge to Cherry Garden is called the Upper Pool. The reach below to Limehouse is the Lower Pool. At this period the majority of trade from Continental and Coastal steamers was lightered from vessels lying at the Tiers.†

Fresh Wharf was a hive of industry, chiefly cargoes from the Mediterranean and the Near East – Turkey, Greece and Alexandria. The Dutch trade was at Custom House and Brewers Quay. Treport steamers at Hay's Wharf load afloat; Ghent steamers to and from Mark Brown's Wharf. A Gravesend trader, *The Witch*, a steam hoy, traded between St Olave's Wharf and Gravesend. There was one tier on the south side, above Tower Bridge – Battle Bridge, chiefly used by steamers from Dunkirk. On the north side the tiers above Tower Bridge were upper and lower Brewers Quay. Mooring chains called Yarmouth Chains just above; this was for small craft, schooners etcetera. Below Tower Bridge to Cherry Garden on the south side, tiers were German Hamburg, Norwoods, Mill Stairs, Upper East Lane, Lower East Lane and Fountain. Except the first mentioned, the principal user was the General Steam Navigation Company with Antwerp, Charente and other continental trade. On the north side, Irongate Buoy (Hull, Yarmouth, Ostend), Dublin Buoy (Jersey), Hermitage Upper, Lower Hermitage and Union Tier (Antwerp, Danzig, Hamburg and Dunkirk trade). Today this trade is done from the docks and wharves with modern jetties and

---

† Buoyed ship moorings

facilities for motor lorry traffic. There is still considerable waterborne business from these ships, but land traffic has competed with us in taking goods direct to the ship's side. Every ship at a Tier had her attendant craft off-loading, or shipping exports. Each landing stairs had regular watermen plying for hire chiefly to and from these ships. Apart from barges, there were rowing boats everywhere in this part of the Pool. Every quay lighterage firm had its boat, and the more important ones had two boat boys. Some, perhaps for economy, had the foreman rowing himself. Everyone knew everybody else. A boat could be recognised long distances away. Some foremen never sat, others huddled. Some would never take an oar, others often spelled the lad or lads when rowing over the tide. The colours of the firms or companies painted on the blades could be recognised and word was soon flashed that 'he' was about. Each firm had its own distinctive whistle. Two foremen in particular were good performers, emitting something like a lark's song would be in quick motion.

The River Police were in row boats, the blades painted white. You could see them in the dark anywhere. These were later painted drab or khaki. In the absence of watermen during the night, the Police would take lightermen off their craft, but this was rather expensive. I had a ride ashore on one occasion with them at the expense of 1/- – my next day's dinner money – the impression being that lightermen worked day and night and were always well breeched. The Customs had their rowing boats. The Surveyor had a four-oared cutter, a real smart turnout. The whole Pool was well served with row boats. Old ropies, beer boats, drudger boats for recovering coal knocked overboard (or borrowing it before that advent), under-watermens' boats for recovering anchors and jetsam.

As we pass under Tower Bridge we look for a passing horse omnibus. Invariably the passenger next to the driver was a member of the fair sex. We would then whistle, 'Mary is young and fair, she rides upon my bus in dear old London.' This was always received as a compliment, the driver saluting by 'dipping the whip'.

The Tower to the Royal Albert Dock

South Devon Wharf just below St Katherine's Dock was the home of trading hoys and sailing craft loading for Margate, Ramsgate and Sandwich. As we near the Wapping entrance of London Dock care is taken to hold our barge up to the point, a hard set to the south'ard takes place here. Just above the point is the site of 'Execution Dock'. I have no authority for stating this except verbal statements from old lightermen when I was a boy. Here, according to their accounts, pirates were executed, the bodies left for three tides to cover (pirates were tough to kill). Pitch and tar was put over the bodies, these being transported by water to Blackwall Point to be suspended from a gibbet as a warning to mariners. On the south side are moorings – Cherry Garden Chains – for several tiers of schooners and ketches. Here the china clay from Cornish ports was discharged into lighters. Then on the same side Church Hole tiers, upper and lower. These were used by large ships from all parts – copper ore, magnesite ore, guano and esparto grass being the usual cargoes. The opposite side, from Tunnel Pier to the Prospect of Whitby (an old pub with overhanging balcony), is known as the Mud Hole, used as an anchorage by sailing barges. This unpleasant incident was witnessed by me off there.

While [I was] rowing past Tunnel Pier with a barge, the body of a drowned person came to the surface with impetus. The arms above the head, slightly bent, gave the appearance of a bow to the river that had taken him, resignation being registered by its movements as it slowly settled into the floating position. 'Deaduns' were a common sight on the riverside. I have been the means of saving life while at work but only getting wet once. Although not as spectacular, a rescue from a dry position, if possible, is the sanest course for rescuer and rescued.

At the end of the Lower Pool the river bends to the right at Cuckold's Point (Cockles). As at all points the tide sets hard away to the bight, a westerly breeze makes the Millwall side a lee shore. Careful nursing here is required to fetch through to where the river again bends left. In the whole of this work the wind was an important factor. Before starting up or down you would form a mental plan, perhaps automatically, of the course to be taken, where to let her fall away to get a wind advantage or where to nurse her up to be right up to windward for the next reach. This part of Rotherhithe with Cockles Point as the apex is or was called 'Down Town'. The waterside inhabitants were called 'Down Towners', families intermarrying for generations. I have been told of people there who only on rare occasions ever left this district for any purpose. Just below the point was the Smallpox Pier where patients were taken by steamer to the floating hospital at Dartford, halfway down Long Reach. There were three of these piers: Fulham, Rotherhithe and Blackwall. On the left bank are the Limehouse entrances to the South and West India Docks. The South West India Dock was originally a canal formed to make a quicker passage avoiding the detour round the 'Isle of Dogs' (City Canal). The vessels lying in these docks are almost all sailing ships, a veritable forest of masts and spars showing right through to Blackwall. These men [are riggers. They] know all the intricate working of the gear of a full rigged ship. The chief trade of sailing vessels from here and the East India Dock was to Australia, New Zealand and San Francisco calling at Chilean ports. Just below the West Dock is Chalkstones Buoys, moorings used by large coasting sailing barges.

We pass Millwall Dock on our left and the Greenland entrance of the Commercial Dock on the right. The river bends left here until we open Blackwall Reach. The tide sets to the south'ard from Millwall Dock to Cubitt Town Point, we working our barge all the time to the north bank. At Cubitt Town we shall allow her to fall over to East Greenwich, thus getting the full run of tide and also to save hard rowing at Blackwall Point. Greenwich College and the Observatory on the hill are on the right bank with the Almshouses just below. Fishing smacks are moored on the foreshore facing the Almshouses, several at this time working from Greenwich. If any sailing barges were underway, now would be the time to see them as live creatures, with all sails drawing on a beam wind, contrasting with the 'gilling' so much detested by the lightermen.

We should, according to the season, have now met pleasure boats either out or homeward bound. In a crowded reach with sailormen tacking and lighters driving, meaning drifting broadside, occasioned by adverse wind, there would be scant room for a large paddle steamer to work through. We always, if apparently in the way under these circumstances, 'squared her up', pulling the lighter stern to the wind, thus presenting the lighter end-on as opposed to broadside. The captain would often come to the end of his bridge and acknowledge the effort with a salute of the hand. Captain Mills of the *London Belle* was a fine type; to see him lift his hand to the right temple and hear, 'thanks old man', in his deep voice, with a holiday cargo of passengers as spectators, was real thanks.

On the Cubitt Town shore right on the point was 'Mouth Organ Wharf' (Grosvenor Wharf). The machinery used in manufacturing block fuel caused weird noises, proving also a good guide in foggy weather.

We now return to Blackwall Reach. On the left side are Folly House buoys. A large fore-and-aft rigged ship is discharging turpentine and resin into lighters. Below here is Yarrow's Yard, several torpedo boats being under construction there. Below this again is Watkins' Hulk, the mooring for the tugs of that firm who in those days used Blackwall as their headquarters. At Blackwall Point the river bends right into Bugsby's Reach.

We are now passing Bow Creek with the Trinity Wharf at one side, the Thames Ironworks opposite. A 'lightship' undergoing repairs would be lying at the Trinity, her name in large white letters painted on her side. At the Ironworks a huge battleship on the stocks towering above any other object (HMS *Albion*). A deafening clattering of rivets being hammered flat would drown other noises. Then Victoria Dock with Cory's dummy the upper side of the entrance. Just a little lower down on the Charlton side were the coal derricks, one and two. Coals were discharged then from ships moored here. If a soft coal was being unloaded, clouds of coal dust would be observed rising. A passing tug running back light to Victoria Dock would have a gang of 'coalies' on her deck, covered in dust, the lips showing red as cherries, the dust having been washed off by the application of the tea bottle, the whites of the eyes also a contrast. If near enough to us we would whistle 'Whist, here comes the bogeyman'. Below the derricks the training ship *Warspite* lay – an old wooden wall. When passing her in the evening and with several lads on her deck they would semaphore to us with their arms, this causing loud laughter among them. Having had no training in semaphore we had to guess the compliments. By whistling, 'A life on the ocean wave', then going through the performance of washing the hands and dropping them smartly palms down, we would try to convey that as sailors they were washouts.

We are now in Woolwich Reach, the dockyard is on our right, the usual wharves on the north bank, iron, chemicals, pickled wood, cable, sugar, stone, flour, old iron, with Foster's beer just above the Ferry. Below the Ferry, the piers of Woolwich Arsenal with the big crane showing boldly and overtopping the wharf, come into view on the south side. The river bends left into Gallions Reach, a favourite anchorage for sailing barges. We must go as near to them as safety allows as our entrance to R A Dock is under the point. This is always a hard slog to get in, with a westerly wind dead out it was real hard work to fetch, but by careful nursing and edging, also by watching all points of gaining ground to avoid the hard set-off, you could make fast at the entrance, watching someone rowing his heart strings out owing to careless shaping for the dock. If in time for the coffee shop, you hoped that your 'two of dripping' would have plenty of gravy on its surface. If not, a glass of sour ginger beer from a tub, a biscuit, cheese and piccalilli or onions.

The 1945 Cowes to Dinard Race

Nigel Sharp

On 9 July 1940, a little over ten months after the outbreak of the Second World War, the Vessels (Immobilisation) Order 1940 came into force. The so-called Phoney War had ended, the miraculous Dunkirk evacuation had taken place, and there was now a very real threat of a German invasion. The main purpose of the Order was to ensure that hostile forces could not make use of any boats lying in tidal waters. Many craft were simply taken away from the water, while others were immobilised in a variety of ways: distributor arms were removed from engines, planks were removed from hulls, and rigs, oars and rudders were carefully hidden away.

In the middle of August, recognising that the greatest danger was in coastal areas, the Port of London Authority's Naval Control Service Officer approved an amendment which allowed permits to be issued for racing dinghies on the Thames upstream of Putney Bridge. Several sailing clubs took full advantage of this throughout the war, organising almost as many races as they would have done in peacetime. Turnouts were smaller, of course, and there were interruptions like the one experienced by Hammersmith's London Corinthian Sailing Club, which cancelled racing for about three months after a V1 flying bomb caused considerable damage to its clubhouse in July 1944.

Sailing was permitted in some other inland areas – at Bardowie Loch, for instance, where the Clyde Cruising Club provided dinghy racing, for which participating members were required to pay an additional annual subscription of £1. West Yorkshire's Yeadon Sailing Club, which had sailed on a reservoir called Yeadon Tam since 1928, was not so lucky. The Avro aeroplane factory and nearby Yeadon Aerodrome, both crucial to the war effort, were just a quarter of a mile away. The Tam would be too clear a landmark for German bombers, so it was drained in 1940.

After the summer of 1943 the threat of invasion was practically non-existent, and the restrictions were slightly relaxed. This relaxation continued over the following two years. Soon after the war in Europe ended in May 1945 almost all constraints were lifted. It is hard to imagine just how desperate the nation's leisure sailors must have been to get back on the water; but to do so was far from straightforward. The vast majority of boats needed a great deal of work to get them seaworthy after six years of neglect. Boatyards were still busy with Admiralty work, and those that did have spare capacity were severely restricted as to what they were allowed do with it. Finally, timber and other materials were in very short supply. Owners of dinghies and other small craft often chose to refit their boats themselves, perhaps with the help of friends, but this was rarely an option for owners of larger boats. In the light of that, a great many clubs decided not to restart their racing programmes until 1946.

One notable exception was the Royal Ocean Racing Club. In November 1940, during the Blitz, the Club's Pall Mall premises had received a direct hit, which had destroyed the buildings and killed the steward. Nothing daunted, by the end of the war the club was settled in its new premises in St James's Place, where it remains today. The Committee decided to organise one offshore race before the end of the 1945 season – a Cowes to Dinard race, one of which had been held in each of the pre-war years since

1930. The 1945 race, the Club decreed, would start on Thursday 13 September 1945.

This was by no means the first post-war keelboat race – the Island Sailing Club's Christchurch Ledge race, for instance, took place on 1 September, attracting eighteen starters, including Uffa Fox sailing one of the airborne lifeboats he had designed and built during the war. Nor would the RORC competitors be the first post-war sailing boats to visit France: on the same day as the Christchurch Ledge race, a Lymington L-Boat called *Shaheen* arrived in Cherbourg Harbour having sailed across the Channel from the Solent. 'In no sense an epic of the sea,' *Shaheen*'s owner, Colonel H G Grace, later wrote, 'but as an incident of contemporary yachting history, it may be a matter of interest to yachtsmen and others perhaps to record what is believed to be the first entrance to a Continental port since the War began, of a private yacht sailing as such from a port in the British Isles.'

In the circumstances, the RORC cannot have expected a big entry. It is perhaps surprising that as many as eight boats made it to the start line, and a great many logistical difficulties had to be overcome to run the race at all. Every boat had its own problems with victualling as well as fitting out, and special arrangements had to be made to overcome problems with passports, Customs officials and currency. Admiralty permission had to be sought on both sides of the Channel (the request was greeted with such enthusiasm by the Commander-in-Chiefs in Portsmouth and Plymouth that they provided the destroyer HMS *Inconstant* to accompany the fleet). Last but not least, the course would involve a considerable diversion around a specially laid mark-boat off Brixham to avoid an extensive minefield in the Channel.

As if all that wasn't enough to deal with, the competitors had to endure very strong southwesterly winds – often reaching gale force – throughout the race. The first retirement was *Windhover*, which, having lost her mast in the Christchurch Ledge race and only been made ready for sea again that very morning, tore her mainsail soon after the start and never left the Solent. Next to go were *Prelude* (just launched the week before 'and then only as a result of strenuous digging by her Sapper crew', it was later reported) and *Amokura*. The boats sought shelter in Poole and Swanage Bay respectively.

In the early hours of Friday morning *Mary Bower* reached the Brixham turning mark, thus winning the £10 prize put up by Brixham Yacht Club. Her crew decided to anchor in the shelter of Torbay for a while, as did, by common consent, each of the four boats which followed. When the conditions abated slightly just before midnight, *Mary Bower* and *Ragna* set off across the Channel, followed in the early hours of Saturday morning by *Windstorm*. The other boats – the Royal Artillery YC's *Marianna* and Owen Aisher's *Yeoman* – decided not to continue.

The difficulties continued on the other side of the Channel, where neither the Casquets or Les Hanois or indeed any of the major Channel Island lights was working. Several French lights were only working irregularly and at low power, and the leading lights into St Malo approaches had all been destroyed.

Mary Bower crossed the finishing line at 2115 on Saturday night in a 'full sail breeze', but the weather deteriorated again soon afterwards. *Ragna* sailed through it, and finished early the following morning. *Windstorm*'s crew, worried that they would not be able to see the Roches Douvres where there was a temporary unlit tower, 'had to heave to and ride out a heavy secondary blow enduring considerable discomfort.' She eventually finished early on Sunday evening. Among her crew was Lieutenant Commander Alfred Miller, a member of the New Zealand NVR who had been in command of HMS *Puffin* on the east coast for three years. 'He will take back to New Zealand the memory of a tough ocean race as well as many hard winter nights on convoy on the East Coast', a *Yachting Monthly* correspondent commented.

Mary Bower added a corrected time victory to her line honours, just as in her inaugural season of 1939, and therefore she retained the King Edward VII Cup. Her crew included her owner,

H S Ashby, her designer Robert Clark, Major E F Parker and Mr Tom Thorneycroft. Parker had also been on board in 1939, and had spent half of the intervening years as a prisoner of war in Germany. *Windstorm*, as the first and only finisher in the Small Class, was awarded the Coupe de Dinard.

There were receptions for the visiting crew members at both the Yacht Club de Dinard and the St Malo Yacht Club. RORC members went some way to repaying the hospitality by 'borrowing' the Dinard club, where they hosted a small cocktail party which was attended by the Assistant British Naval attaché who had 'made the very trying twelve hour journey from Paris'.

In the November issue of *Yachting World* there was a detailed report of the race, in which a correspondent wrote that the three finishers 'had the satisfaction of passing a severe test of seamanship, to be rewarded by the warm reception they received from the people of France on completion of the race.' As for HMS *Inconstant*, he noted that 'fortunately her duties proved light, though she spent some anxious moments trying to keep track of eight small craft scattered by a gale over a very wide area.' He also reported that St Malo had been 'largely devastated by fire as a result of the desultory shelling of the town a year ago.' But the report finished on a positive note when it said 'there is no doubt that the race has done a great deal of good on both sides of the Channel. It has brought home to our friends in France the fact that peace reigns once more and the question as to whether it is possible to hold a race at all has been settled.'

Yachting Monthly's January 1946 issue included a piece by racing correspondent John Scott Hughes in which he expressed 'nothing but admiration for the skill and stamina of those who took part', but also criticised the RORC for holding the race in such conditions. 'What the sea was like in the Needles Channel only the eight competitors and the lighthouse keepers saw,' he wrote, apparently under the impression that the race had started in a very strong west-going tide, 'but it can be imagined'.

This prompted a response in the following issue from J H C

Morris, who had raced on board *Mary Bower* and who thought Hughes had 'put his foot in it in his remarks about the Cowes-Dinard race'. He clarified the tide issue by pointing out that it was 'two days off dead neaps' and had not started running west until some time after the start. Conditions in the Needles Channel had not been too bad: 'we got wet, of course, but who expects to keep dry in an ocean race?' He also challenged Hughes's view that the race could have been cut short at Torbay, after which 'actually we had a lovely sail, with sheets eased, and no drop of water came over the side the whole way over.' He finished by pointing out that the Yacht Club de Dinard would have been extremely disappointed if no boats had finished the race, as it 'had laid on a most sumptuous entertainment for our benefit, which involved putting by out of their rations for many weeks.'

The RORC has run the Cowes to Dinard race every year since, with substantially greater entries – up to fifty-eight as soon as 1947, for instance. In 2013 there were almost a hundred.

Hammond Innes – a Memoir

John Lang

Like most people, I sometimes dream up mental shortlists of books I would like to have with me on a desert island. One book that seems to feature in every list is *Maddon's Rock* by Hammond Innes.

It is first and foremost a wonderful adventure story about a man fighting to clear his name, a ship, skulduggery and a lonely, storm-lashed rock in the Arctic Ocean, full of suspense and with a very satisfactory ending. It has a special place in my heart for a different reason: it was given to me by the author in October 1951. I was ten at the time, and although I did not know it then, it was the beginning of a friendship that lasted forty-five years.

Ralph Hammond Innes was a prolific author who wrote some thirty novels, travel and children's books between the late 1930s and his death in 1998. In 1937, he married a cousin of my naval officer father, the actress Dorothy Lang. Among the great excitements of my childhood were occasional invitations to go sailing with Ralph in his 39′ Bermudan cutter *Triune of Troy*.

His working technique was to explore the wilder parts of the world in the hope that an idea for a story would emerge from his experience. His first journey was to the Persian Gulf at the invitation of my father, who was commanding the Bahrain-based Black Swan class frigate HMS *Flamingo.* He spent some three weeks embarked in *Flamingo,* and was to write later that the Gulf was like 'a shallow pot of salt water simmering everlastingly in the sun's fire.' Anyone travelling to the Gulf today might find some of his observations about the pre-oil-boom era interesting. He noted, for instance, that the bar across the entrance to the creek at Dubai, which nowadays has two mighty ports, was so silted up that dhows had difficulty getting in.

Nearly all Hammond Innes novels show men battling against raw nature. He was at his best when writing about the sea, drawing heavily on his time spent racing and cruising, and took every opportunity to take passage in larger vessels – army landing craft, deep sea trawlers and Norwegian whalecatchers.

During his life he owned three boats. The first, *Sonia,* was wonderful for pottering about in an estuary but was unsuitable for anything more adventurous, and was replaced by *Triune of Troy.* She was always too tender and wet for comfort, and he set his heart on something more suitable for long-distance cruising. The result was the steel-hulled sloop *Mary Deare,* named after an early nineteenth-century Bristol-built pirate ship carrying gold which was allegedly buried on the uninhabited island of Cocos some 340 miles off the Costa Rican coast. He used the subject in one of his children's books *Cocos Gold.* The name became better known when it featured in *The Wreck of the 'Mary Deare'.* Some of the passages in the book are among the best descriptions of life at sea in contemporary literature.

Hammond Innes strove for accuracy, and his time spent afloat did much to ensure he achieved it. Once in a while however he found himself trying to write about something he had little or no experience of and, in 1960, I recall him asking me about life on a merchant ship and also in Singapore. (I had embarked on the first stage of a seagoing career, and was sailing as a navigating officer cadet with the P&O Steam Navigation Company and had just completed two voyages to the Far East.) It wasn't until some years later that I discovered he had been working on the novel *The Strode Venturer* about a merchant ship and the Maldive islands. I have severe doubts that anything I told him about the delights of cleaning out number two hold in the middle of the South China Sea did much for his research, but I was thrilled to be asked.

It wasn't until long after I had transferred from the P&O to the Royal Navy that our paths crossed again. In the mid-1980s I had the supreme good fortune to command, as a captain, the Type 22 frigate HMS *Beaver,* and we were on our way back to the UK having undertaken some trials in the Mediterranean. I sought approval to embark Ralph for the final few days of the deployment. Approval was readily granted, and he embarked in Lisbon for the passage home to the English Channel and Devonport.

He took a great interest in everyone and everything on board but particularly enjoyed his time on the bridge with the officer of the watch. About two years later he wrote to me again, and asked if I would cast my eye over the typescript of *Medusa,* a new novel he was writing about an obsolete frigate in the Mediterranean that was ordered to become a sitting duck for the enemy. He said that many of his readers were ex-Navy and sticklers for accuracy. (He added, helpfully, that he had been having dinner with a former First Sea Lord a few nights earlier.) In the course of time, I was delighted to discover he had dedicated the book to both me and my father.

He died aged eighty-four in 1998. I was touched to be asked to read one of the lessons at his thanksgiving service held in London, and even more so to learn that I was a beneficiary in his will. Not unnaturally I took an interest in the other beneficiaries, and noted that the greater part of his estate was being left to an organisation called the Association of Sail Training Organisations. It was not until four years after Ralph's death that a chance encounter with the then chairman of ASTO revealed more about his great interest in sail training. He had been vice president of the Association, and had sailed in both the Sea Cadet's brig *Royalist* and, like me, the Sail Training Association's *Sir Winston Churchill.* He had seen how youth from all walks of life could benefit from a few days at sea under sail, away from their familiar comfort zones.

Some months later I was approached by the Hon Secretary of ASTO and asked if I would consider becoming its President. I would like to think that had he been alive today, Ralph Hammond Innes would have been thrilled that the ten-year-old boy to whom he had given one of his books many years ago was continuing to support his passion for bringing adventure and life-changing experiences to the young and disabled of our country.

The 'Mary Deare' †

Hammond Innes

I was tired and very cold; a little scared, too. The red and green navigation lights cast a weird glow over the sails. Beyond was nothing, a void of utter darkness in which the sea made little rushing noises. I eased my cramped legs, sucking on a piece of barley sugar. Above me the sails swung in a ghostly arc, slatting back and forth as *Sea Witch* rolled and plunged. There was scarcely wind enough to move the boat through the water, yet the swell kicked up by the March gales ran as strong as ever and my numbed brain was conscious all the time that this was only a lull. The weather forecast at six o'clock had been ominous. Winds of gale force were reported imminent in sea areas Rockall, Shannon, Sole and Finisterre. Beyond the binnacle light the shadowy outline of the boat stretched ahead of me, merging into the clammy blackness of the night. I had dreamed of this moment so often. But it was March and now, after fifteen hours at sea in the Channel, the excitement of owning our own boat was gone, eaten up by the cold. The glimmer of a breaking wave appeared out of the darkness and slapped against the counter, flinging spray

† Adapted from *The Wreck of the 'Mary Deare'*, Vintage Classics 2013

in my face and sidling off into the blackness astern with a hiss of white water. God! It was cold! Cold and clammy – and not a star anywhere.

The door of the charthouse slammed back to give me a glimpse of the lit saloon. Against it loomed Mike Duncan's oilskin-padded bulk, holding a steaming mug in either hand. The door slammed to again, shutting out the lit world below, and the darkness and the sea crowded in. 'Soup?' Mike's cheerful, freckled face appeared abruptly out of the night, hanging disembodied in the light from the binnacle. He handed me a mug. 'Nice and fresh up here after the galley,' he said. Then the smile was wiped from his face. 'What the hell's that?' He was staring past my left shoulder, at something astern of us on the port quarter. 'Can't be the moon, can it?'

I swung round. A cold green translucence showed at the edge of visibility. The light grew steadily brighter, phosphorescent and unearthly – a ghastly brilliance, like a bloated glow-worm. Then suddenly it condensed and hardened into a green pinpoint, and I yelled at Mike: 'The Aldis – quick!' It was the starboard navigation light of a big steamer, and it was bearing straight down on us. Her deck lights were appearing now, misted and yellow; and gently, like the muffled beat of a tom-tom, the sound of her engines reached out to us in a low, pulsating throb.

The beam of the Aldis lamp stabbed the night, blinding us with the reflected glare from a thick blanket of mist. It was a sea mist that had crept up on me in the dark without my knowing it. The white of a bow wave showed dimly in the brilliance, and then the shadowy outline of the bows themselves took shape. In an instant I could see the whole for'ard half of the ship. It was like a ghost ship emerging out of the mist, and the blunt bows were already towering over us as I swung the wheel.

It seemed an age that I watched *Sea Witch* turn, waiting for the jib to fill on the other tack and bring her head round, and all the time I could hear the surge of that bow wave coming nearer. 'She's going to hit us! Christ! She's going to hit us!' I can still hear Mike's cry, high and strident in the night. He was blinking the Aldis, directing the beam straight at her bridge. The whole superstructure was lit up, the light reflecting back in flashes from the glass windows. And the towering mass of the steamer kept on coming, thundering down on us at a good 8 knots without any alteration of course.

The main and mizzen booms swung over with a crash. The jib was aback now. I left it like that for a moment, watching her head pay off. Every detail of *Sea Witch*, from the tip of her long bowsprit to the top of her mainmast, was lit by the green glow of the starboard light, now high above us. I let go the port jib sheet, hauling in on the starboard sheet, saw the sail fill, and then Mike screamed, 'Hold on!' There was a great roaring sound and a wall of white water hit us. It swept over the cockpit, lifting me out of my seat, tugging at my grip on the wheel. The sails swung in a crazy arc; they swung so far that the boom and part of the mainsail were buried for a moment in the back of a wave. Tons of water spilled across our decks; and close alongside the steamer slid by like a cliff.

Slowly *Sea Witch* righted herself as the water poured off her in a white foam. Mike was clutching the backstay runner, shouting obscenities at the top of his voice. His words came to me as a frail sound against the solid thumping of the ship's engines. And then another sound emerged out of the night – the steady thrashing of a propeller partly clear of the water.

I shouted to Mike, but he had already realised the danger and had switched the Aldis on again. Its brilliant light showed us plates pitted deep with rust and a weed-grown Plimsoll mark high above the water. Then the plates curved up to the stern and we could see the propeller blades slashing the water into a swirling froth. *Sea Witch* trembled, sails slack. Then she slid off the back of a wave into that millrace and the blades were whirling close along our port side, churning white water over the cabin top, flinging it up into the mainsail. It was like that for a moment. Then they flailed off into the darkness beyond the bowsprit and we were left pitching in the broken water of the ship's wake. The Aldis beam picked out her name: *MARY DEARE* – SOUTHAMPTON. We stared dazedly at her rust-streaked lettering while the stern became shadowy, then vanished abruptly. Only the beat of her engines remained then, throbbing gently and gradually dying away into the night. 'Bastards!' Mike shouted, suddenly finding his voice. 'Bastards!'

The door of the charthouse slid back, and a figure emerged. It was Hal. 'Are you boys all right?' His voice – a little too calm, a little too cheerful – shook slightly.

'Didn't you see what happened?' Mike cried. 'They must have seen us. I was shining the Aldis straight at the bridge. If they'd been keeping a lookout –'

'I don't think they were keeping a lookout. In fact, I don't think there was anybody on the bridge.'

It was said so quietly that for a moment I didn't realise the implication. 'How do you mean?'

He came out onto the deck then. 'It was just before the bow wave hit us. I knew something was wrong and I'd got as far as the charthouse. I found myself looking out through the window along the beam of the Aldis lamp. It was shining right on to the bridge. I don't think there was anybody there.'

I said, 'Do you realise what you're saying?'

'Yes, of course, I do.' His tone was peremptory, a little military. Hal was an ex-Gunner, a Colonel retired, who spent most of the summer months ocean racing. He had a lot of experience of the sea. 'It's odd, isn't it?'

We didn't say anything for a moment. I think we were all too astonished. The idea of a big ship ploughing her way through the rock-infested sea so close to the French coast without anybody at the helm . . . It was absurd.

Mike's voice broke the silence. 'What happened to those mugs of soup?' The beam of the Aldis lamp clicked on, revealing the mugs lying in a foot of water at the bottom of the cockpit. 'I'd better go and make another brew.' And then to Hal who was standing, half-dressed, his body braced against the charthouse: 'What about you, Colonel?'

Hal nodded. He watched Mike until he had gone below and

then turned to me. 'How did we come to be right across her bows like that?'

I explained that the ship had been downwind from us and we hadn't heard the beat of her engines. 'The first we saw of her was her starboard navigation light coming at us.'

'No fog signal?'

'We didn't hear one.'

'Odd!' He came aft and seated himself beside me on the cockpit coaming. 'Had a look at the barometer?' he asked.

'No,' I said. 'What's it doing?'

'Going down. You know, this gale could come up on us pretty quickly.' I didn't say anything and he pulled his pipe out and began to suck on it. 'I tell you frankly, John, I don't like it. If the forecast turns out right and the wind backs northwesterly, then we'll be on a lee shore. I don't like gales and I don't like lee shores, particularly when the lee shore is the Channel Islands.'

I thought he wanted me to put back to the French coast and I didn't say anything; just sat there staring at the compass card, feeling obstinate and a little scared.

'It's a pity about the kicker,' he murmured. 'If the kicker hadn't packed up we'd be halfway across the Channel by now.'

'I'm not putting back.'

He took his pipe out of his mouth as though to say something, then put it back.

'The real trouble is that you're not used to sailing in a boat that hasn't been kept up to ocean racing pitch.' I hadn't meant to say that.

An awkward silence fell between us. At length he stopped sucking on his pipe. 'It's only that I like to arrive,' he said quietly. 'The rigging is rusty, the ropes rotten and the sails –'

'We went over all that in Morlaix,' I said. 'Plenty of yachts cross the Channel in worse shape than *Sea Witch*.'

'Not in March with a gale warning. And not without an engine.' He got up and went for'ard as far as the mast, bending down and hauling at something. There was the sound of splintering wood.

He came back and tossed a section of the bulwarks into the cockpit at my feet. 'The bow wave did that.'

'I told you, I'm having her surveyed as soon as we reach Lymington.'

'Yes, but that doesn't help us now. If this gale comes up on us suddenly . . . I'm a prudent mariner.'

'I can't afford to be prudent,' I said. 'Not right now.'

Mike and I had just formed a small salvage company, and every day we delayed getting the boat to England for conversion was a day lost out of our diving season. Hal knew that.

'Close-hauled we can just about lay Hanois on Guernsey,' he said. 'We'll then be in a position to take advantage of the wind when it backs and run for shelter to Peter Port.'

I rubbed my hand over my eyes. I was tired and the steamer incident had left me badly shaken. It was queer, the way the vessel had sailed right through us like that.

'It won't help your salvage venture if you smash the boat up.' Hal had taken my silence for refusal. 'Apart from the gear, we're not very strongly crewed.'

'Very well,' I said. 'We'll head for Guernsey.'

He nodded as though he'd known it all along. 'You'll need to steer north 65° east then.'

I turned the wheel and watched the compass card swing to the new course. He must have been working it out in the charthouse just before the steamer came up on us. 'I take it you worked out the distance, too?'

'Fifty-four miles.'

An uneasy silence settled between us. I could hear him sucking at his empty pipe, but I kept my eyes on the compass and didn't look at him. I should have thought of Peter Port for myself. But there'd been so much to do at Morlaix getting the boat ready . . . I'd just about worked myself to a standstill before ever we put to sea.

His voice came out of the darkness at my side, a little hesitant. 'You know, if there really was nobody on board that ship . . .' He checked and then added, half-jokingly, 'That would have been a piece of salvage that would have set you up for life.' He shrugged his shoulders and laughed. 'Well, I think I'll turn in again now.' He got up and his 'good night' floated back to me from the dark gap of the charthouse.

The blackness of the night closed round me. Could there really have been nobody on the bridge? It was too fantastic. And yet, cold and alone, with the pale glimmer of the sails swooping above me and the dismal dripping of the mist condensed on the canvas, anything seemed possible.

At three Hal relieved me and for two hours I slept, dreaming of blunt, rusted bows hanging over us, toppling slowly, everlastingly. And in an instant I was being shaken and was stumbling out to the helm in the brain-numbing hour before the dawn.

Daylight came slowly, a reluctant dawn that showed a drab, sullen sea heaving gently, the steepness flattened out of the swell. The wind was northerly now, but still light; and some time during the night we had gone over on to the other tack.

At ten to seven Hal and I were in the charthouse for the weather report. The forecast for our own area of Portland was: 'wind light, northerly at first, backing north-westerly later and increasing strong to gale'. Hal glanced at me, but said nothing. There was no need. I checked our position, then gave Mike the course to steer for Peter Port.

It was a queer morning. There was a lot of scud about and by the time we had finished breakfast it was moving across the sky quite fast. Yet at sea level there was scarcely any wind so that, with full main and mizzen set and the big yankee jib, we were creeping through the water at a bare 3 knots, rolling sluggishly. There was still a mist of sorts and visibility wasn't much more than two miles.

We didn't talk much. I think we were all three of us too conscious of the sea's menace. Peter Port was still thirty miles away. The silence and the lack of wind was oppressive. 'I'll go and check our position again,' I said. Hal nodded as though the thought had been in his mind, too.

But poring over the chart didn't help. As far as I could tell we were six miles north-northwest of the Roches Douvres, that huddle of rocks and submerged reefs that is the western outpost of the Channel Islands. But I couldn't be certain; my dead reckoning depended too much on tide and leeway.

And then Mike knocked the bottom out of my calculations. 'There's a rock about two points on the starboard bow,' he called to me. 'A big one sticking up out of the water.'

I grabbed the glasses and flung out of the charthouse. 'Where?' My mouth was suddenly harsh and dry. If it were the Roches Douvres, then we must have been set down a good deal farther than I thought. And it couldn't be anything else; it was all open sea between Roches Douvres and Guernsey. 'Where?' I repeated.

'Over there!' Mike was pointing.

I screwed up my eyes. But I couldn't see anything. The clouds had thinned momentarily and a queer sun-glow was reflected on the oily surface of the sea, merging it with the moisture-laden atmosphere. There was no horizon; at the edge of visibility sea and air became one. I searched through the glasses. 'I can't see it,' I said. 'How far away?'

'I don't know. I've lost it now. But it wasn't more than a mile.'

'You're sure it was a rock?'

'What else could it be?' He was staring into the distance, his eyes narrowed against the luminous glare of the haze. 'It was a big rock with some sort of tower or pinnacle in the middle of it.'

The Roches Douvres light! I glanced at Hal seated behind the wheel. 'We'd better alter course,' I said. 'The tide is setting us down at about 2 knots.' My voice sounded tense. If it was the Roches Douvres and the wind fell any lighter, we could be swept right down on to the reef.

He nodded and swung the wheel. 'That would put you out by five miles in your dead reckoning.'

'Yes.'

He had taken his sou'wester off and his grey hair, standing on end, gave his face a surprised, puckish look. 'I think you're underrating yourself as a navigator, but you're the boss. How much do you want me to bear up?'

'Two points at least.'

'There's an old saying,' he murmured: 'The prudent mariner, when in doubt, should assume his dead reckoning to be correct.' He looked at me with a quizzical lift to his bushy eyebrows. 'We don't want to miss Guernsey, you know.'

A mood of indecision took hold of me. Maybe it was just the strain of the long night, but I wasn't sure what to do for the best.

'Did you see it?' I asked him.

'No.'

I turned to Mike and asked him again whether he was sure it was a rock he'd seen.

'You can't be sure of anything in this light.'

'But you definitely saw something?'

'Yes. And it had some sort of a tower on it.'

'Then it must be the Roches Douvres,' I murmured.

'Look!' Mike cried. 'Over there.'

I followed the line of his outstretched arm. On the edge of visibility, lit by the sun's pale gleam, was the outline of a flattish rock with a light tower in the middle. I had the glasses on it immediately, but it was no more than a reddish tint glimmering through the golden haze. I dived into the charthouse and snatched up the chart, staring at the shape of the Roches Douvres reef. It marked drying rock outcrops for a full mile northwest of the 92' light tower. We must be right on the fringe of those outcrops. 'Steer north,' I shouted to Hal, 'and sail her clear just as fast as you can.'

'Aye, aye, skipper.' He swung the wheel, calling to Mike to trim the sheets. He was looking over his shoulder at the Roches Douvres light as I came out of the charthouse. 'You know,' he said, 'there's something odd here. I know the Channel Islands pretty well and I've never seen any rock that showed up red like that.'

I steadied myself against the charthouse and focused the glasses on it again. The gleam of sunlight had become more positive. Visibility was improving all the time. I saw it clearly then, and I was almost laughing with relief. 'It's not a rock,' I said. 'It's a ship.'

There was no doubt about it now. The rusty hull was no longer blurred, but stood out clear and sharp, and what I had taken to be a light tower was its single funnel.

We were all of us laughing with the sense of relief as we turned back on to the course. 'Hove-to, by the look of it,' Mike said.

It certainly looked like it, for now that we were back on course her position didn't seem to have altered at all. She was lying broadside-on to us, as though held there by the wind. As we closed with her and her outline became clearer, I could see that she was stationary, wallowing in the swell. Our course would leave her about half a mile to starboard. I reached for the glasses. There was something about the ship; something about her shape and her rusty hull and the way she seemed a little down at the bows.

'Probably pumping out her bilges,' Hal said, his voice hesitant as though he, too, were puzzled.

I focused the glasses and the outline of the vessel leaped towards me. She was an old boat, with straight bows and a clean sweep to her sheer. She had an old-fashioned counter stern, an untidy clutter of derricks round her masts, and too much superstructure. Her single smokestack was almost vertical. At one time she had been painted black, but now she had a rusty, uncared-for look. There was a sort of lifelessness about her that held me with the glasses to my eyes. And then I saw the lifeboat.

'Steer straight for her, will you, Hal?' I said.

'Anything wrong?'

'One of the lifeboats is hanging vertically from its davits.' It was more than that. The other davits were empty. I passed him the glasses. 'Take a look.'

Soon we could see the empty davits with the naked eye, and the single lifeboat hanging from the falls. 'Looks deserted,' Mike said. 'And she's quite a bit down by the bows. Do you think . . . ?' He left the sentence unfinished. The same thought was in all our minds.

We came down on her amidships. The name at her bows was so broken up with rust streaks that we couldn't read it. Close-to she looked in wretched shape. Her rusty bow plates were out of true, her superstructure was damaged and she was definitely down by the bows. A festoon of wires hung from her mast derricks. She looked as though she'd taken a hell of a hammering.

We went about within a cable's length of her and I hailed her through our megaphone. My voice lost itself in the silence of the sea. There was no answer. The only sound was the sloshing of the swell against her sides. We ran down on her quickly then, Hal steering to pass close under her stern. I think we were all of us watching for her name. And then suddenly there it was in rust-streaked lettering high above our heads, just as it had been during the night: *MARY DEARE* – SOUTHAMPTON.

She was quite a big boat, at least 6000 tons. Abandoned like that, she should have had a salvage tug in attendance, ships standing by. But there wasn't another vessel in sight. She was alone and lifeless within twenty miles of the French coast. I glanced up along her starboard side as we came out from under her stern. Both davits were empty, the lifeboats gone.

'You were right,' Mike said. 'There wasn't anybody on the bridge last night.'

We stared up at her in silence as we slipped away from her. The rope falls hung forlornly from the empty davits. A thin trail of smoke from her funnel was the only sign of life. 'They must have abandoned ship just before they nearly ran us down,' I said.

'But she was steaming full ahead,' Hal said, more to himself than to us. 'You don't abandon ship with the engines going full ahead. And why didn't she radio for help?'

I was thinking of what Hal had said half-jokingly last night. If there was really nobody on board . . . I stood there, my hands braced on the guardrail, searching for some sign of life. There was nothing; nothing but that thin wisp of smoke trailing from the funnel. Salvage! A ship of 6000tons, drifting and abandoned. It was unbelievable. And if we could bring her into port under her own steam . . . I turned to Hal. 'Do you think you could lay *Sea Witch* alongside her, close enough for me to get hold of one of those falls?'

'Don't be a fool,' he said. 'There's still quite a swell running. You may damage the boat, and if this gale–'

But I was in no mood for caution now. 'Ready about!' I called. 'Lee ho!' We came about on to the other tack. 'We'll jog up to her close-hauled,' I told Hal. 'I'll jump for the ropes as you go about.'

'It's crazy,' he said. 'You've a hell of a height to climb to the deck. And supposing the wind pipes up. I may not be able to get you –'

'To hell with the wind!' I cried. 'Do you think I'm going to pass up a chance like this? This is a one in a lifetime.'

He stared at me for a moment, then nodded. 'It's your boat.' We were headed back for the ship now. 'When we get under her lee,' Hal said, 'we'll be pretty well blanketed. I may have some difficulty –' He stopped there and glanced up at the burgee.

I had done the same. There was a different feel about the boat now. She was surging along with a noise of water from her bows and spray wetting the foredeck. The burgee was streamed out to starboard. I checked with the compass. 'You'll have no difficulty standing off from her,' I said. 'The wind's northwesterly now.'

He nodded, his eyes lifting to the sails. 'You're still determined to go on board?'

'Yes.'

'Well, you'd better not stay long. There's some weight in the wind.'

'I'll be as quick as I can,' I said. We were doing all of 4 knots and the ship was coming up fast. I went to the charthouse door and yelled to Mike. He came almost immediately. 'We'll go about just before we get to her. That'll take the way off her and you'll be all set to stand off again.' I was stripping off my oilskins. Already, the rusty sides of the *Mary Deare* were towering above us. It looked a hell of a height to climb. 'Ready about?' I asked.

'Ready about,' Hal said. He swung the wheel. *Sea Witch* began to pay off, slowly, very slowly. For a moment it looked as though she was going to poke her long bowsprit through the steamer's rusty plates. Then she was round.

There was little wind now that we were close under the *Mary*

Deare. The sails flapped lazily. The crosstrees were almost scraping the steamer's sides as we rolled in the swell. I ran to the mast, climbed the starboard rail and stood there, poised, my feet on the bulwarks, my hands gripping the shrouds. Her way carried me past the for'ard davit falls. There was still a gap of several yards between me and the ship's side. Hal closed it slowly. Leaning out, I watched the after davit falls slide towards me. There was a jar as the tip of our crosstrees rammed the plates above my head. The first of the falls came abreast of me. I leaned right out, but they were a good foot beyond my reach. 'This time!' Hal shouted. The crosstrees jarred again. I felt the jolt of it through the shroud I was clinging to. And then my hand closed on the ropes and I let go, falling heavily against the ship's side, the lift of a swell wetting me to my knees. 'Okay!' I yelled. I hauled myself upwards with desperate urgency. There was the slam of wood just below my feet. Then I saw *Sea Witch* was clear, standing out away from the ship.

'Don't be long,' Hal shouted. *Sea Witch* was already heeling to the wind, the water creaming back from her bows, a white wake showing at her stern as she gathered speed.

I began to climb.

The Instruments of Navigation

Christopher Schüler

'For cartography', wrote the Alexandrian geographer and astronomer Claudius Ptolemy in the second century AD, 'it is necessary to consider the outward appearance and magnitude of the earth, to discover under which of the heavenly spheres its various parts lie.' Since earliest times, people have gazed at the night sky and seen that the stars formed recognisable patterns. With repeated observation, it gradually became clear that the whole celestial panoply rotated through the heavens in a regular and predictable manner, making the sky both a calendar and an aid to direction.

Seven-tenths of our planet is covered by water. To find their way across its expanses, on which there are no landmarks to show the way, sailors turned to the stars. In ancient times, seafarers calculated their latitude using the simplest of methods – the breadth of a finger, the height of a thumb – to measure the altitude of a star above the horizon. To find their way home, they needed only to head north or south until the star appeared at its original altitude, turn east or west, and sail down the latitude, keeping the star at a constant height. By a strange paradox it was therefore necessary to map the heavens before it was possible to map the ocean.

Astronomy, like so much else in civilisation, began with the ancient Babylonians in Mesopotamia, the land between the Tigris and Euphrates that is now Iraq. Cuneiform tablets inscribed with astronomical tables have been found throughout the region. The ancient Egyptians were also familiar with the movements of the stars and planets: the temples at Philae and Dendera are oriented to the heliacal rising of Sirius, and tomb decorations in the Valley of the Kings depict celestial diagrams and stellar clocks.

While ancient sailors generally hugged the coasts and therefore had little need for celestial navigation, the Minoans of Crete ventured as far as the island of Thera and to Egypt. Such journeys would have taken more than a day across open water, requiring them to navigate by the stars, particularly the constellation Ursa Major (the Great Bear). Their palace at Knossos is oriented so that at the spring and autumn equinoxes the first rays of sun strike a concave stone in the floor; while the walls of the hilltop sanctuaries at Zakros are aligned to facilitate observations of the rising and setting of the star Arcturus.

The first written record of navigation by the stars occurs in Homer's *Odyssey,* where Odysseus, leaving Calypso's island, charts his course by the Great Bear which, 'the beautiful goddess had bidden him to keep on the left hand as he sailed over the sea.' Factual accounts of actual journeys by ancient Greeks survive in the form of *periploi* – 'circumnavigations' – listing the ports and coastal landmarks, with intermediate distances, that the captain of a vessel would find along a shore.

In the sixth century BC, the Carthaginian explorer Hanno the Navigator described the coast of Africa from present-day Morocco as far south as the Gulf of Guinea. Alexander the Great's admiral Nearchos left a detailed record of his naval voyage from India to Susa in Persia 326BC. At around the same time, the Greek traveller Pytheas, navigating by the sun and the Pole Star, sailed from Marseilles to reach Britain and the northern ocean. The *Periplus of the Erythraean Sea,* written by a Romanised Alexandrian in the first century AD, details the shoreline from the Red

Sea to the coast of India as far as the Ganges and the east coast of Africa, while Arrian's *Periplus Ponti Euxini* describes the trade routes along the coasts of the Black Sea.

According to Cicero in his *De Re Publica,* Archimedes built a machine composed of spheres that displayed the motions of the sun and moon, the five planets known at the time, and solar and lunar eclipses. Cicero also mentions another such device built by his friend Posidonius of Rhodes (c. 135-51BC):

> each one of the revolutions of which brings about the same movement in the Sun and Moon and five wandering stars [planets] as is brought about each day and night in the heavens.

The Antikythera mechanism, a complex machine of bronze gears recovered from the Aegean in 1900, is thought to be a similar device.

The astronomical and geographical knowledge of the ancient world was systematised and expanded by Ptolemy in the first half of the second century AD. But with the collapse of classical civilisation in Europe, much of this information was lost to the West. Astronomy came to a standstill in Europe, and what shipping there was tended to hug the coasts – with the exception of the Vikings who, navigating by the sun, reached Iceland in the ninth century, Greenland in 986, and Newfoundland around the year 1000.

Astronomy and cartography, like much of the science of classical antiquity, were kept alive by Islamic scholars, and found their way back to western Europe in the later Middle Ages in Latin translations from the Arabic. The *Tabula Rogeriana,* a world map created by the Muslim cartographer Muhammad Al-Idrisi in 1154 for the Norman King Roger II of Sicily, represents the summation of centuries of Arab cartography. Based on extensive interviews with travellers, it was far more realistic than contemporary Western maps such as the Hereford *Mappa Mundi,* and remained the most accurate depiction of the world for the next three hundred years.

It may have been the introduction of the magnetic compass

from China, via the Islamic world, in the twelfth century that emboldened European sailors to cast off into uncharted waters once more. In the following century, Alfonso the Wise of Castile ordered charts and compasses for the use of his shipmasters. Soon afterwards, portolan charts began to be made, first by Jewish cartographers in Majorca and then in Italy. These marine charts, usually drawn on to a whole sheet of vellum, showed the coasts in considerable detail, leaving inland areas blank. The seas were criss-crossed with rhumbs – diagonal lines emanating from the thirty-two points of the compass to enable mariners to chart a course to their destination.

Beside the compass, the instruments of navigation available to Renaissance mariners consisted of an astrolabe, quadrant or cross-staff to determine latitude by the altitude of the sun or pole star; a plumb line to take depth soundings; and a nocturnal to calculate the time at night by the position of the stars. To use these instruments, mariners needed to know the position of the sun and stars on any given date, so seamen's manuals included an almanac or tables providing this information for years ahead. At the end of the sixteenth century, the English mariner John Davis (c. 1550-1605) improved on the cross-staff, inventing a back-staff that avoided the need to look into the sun – and sharpened the instrument's accuracy – by using an arc-shaped quadrant to cast a shadow on the edge of the rod. Also known as the Davis quadrant, the back-staff continued in use well into the eighteenth century.

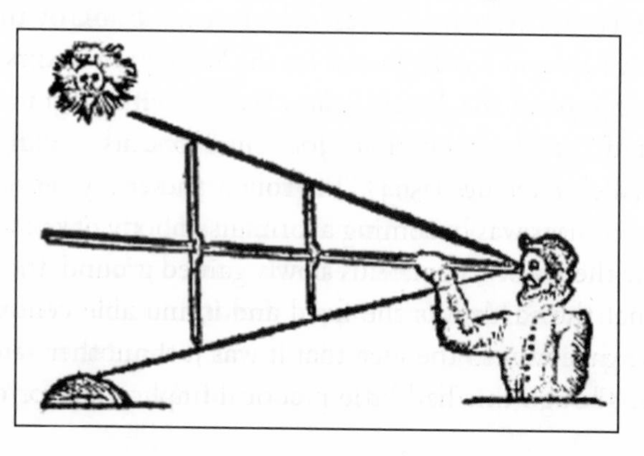

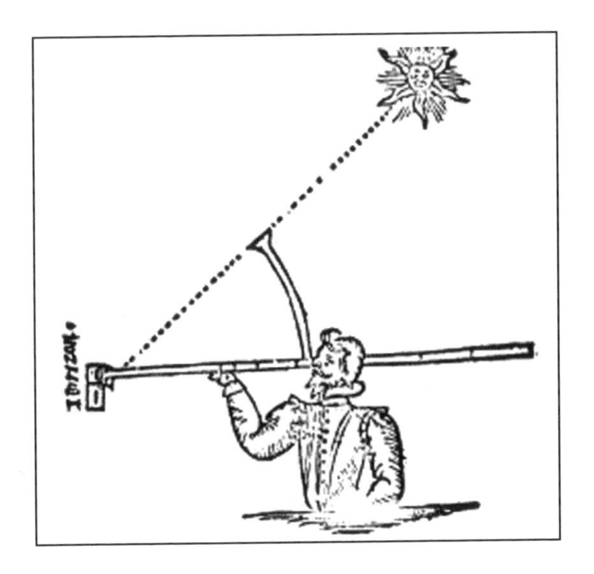

These two woodcuts from John Davis's The Seaman's Secrets *(London, 1607) depict a seaman finding his latitude by measuring the altitude of the sun with traditional cross-staff (below opposite) and with Davis's improved back-staff (above). The operator stands with his back to the sun, so that the arc quadrant casts a shadow on to the calibrated staff to give a reading of the latitude.*

A plethora of printed handbooks on the geometrical aspects of navigation appeared, including Pedro de Medina's *Arte de Navegar* (1545), Martín Cortés de Albacar's book of the same title (1551), Bourne's *A Regiment for the Sea* (1574), Thomas Fale's *Horologiographia: The Art of Dialling* (1593) – with diagrams by the celebrated Dutch cartographer Jodocus Hondius – and Thomas Blundeville's *Exercises* (1594). The rough and ready reckoning of earlier centuries was becoming a formalised body of knowledge.

As the theory of Copernicus slowly gained ground, the ancient belief that the earth was the fixed and immutable centre of the universe gave way to the idea that it was just another satellite of the sun. Though this had little practical implication for celestial navigation, cartographers began to emancipate themselves from the legacy of Ptolemy, superseding his tables of coordinates with the newer, more accurate readings of contemporary mariners, and experimenting with alternatives to his conical projection. In 1569, Gerardus Mercator devised the cylindrical projection that bears his name and would hold sway for centuries. Like many cartographers of his age, Mercator was driven by a thirst for knowledge, but his new projection also had a practical purpose, as the full title of his map, *Nova et Aucta Orbis Terrae Descriptio ad Usum Navigantium Emendata* – 'a new and augmented description of Earth corrected for the use of sailors' – makes clear.

As the precision of the instruments of navigation increased, so too did the accuracy of sea charts. Marine atlases began to be printed. In addition to charts, they contained practical advice on the use of instruments, often following the format of the old manuscript manuals, with a section on the spheres followed by astronomical tables and descriptions of the instruments. The first and most successful was the *Spieghel der Zeevaerdt* (1584) by Lucas Waghenhaer, a Dutch pilot based at Enkhuizen. Waghenhaer's manual became so popular that English sailors referred to any sea chart as a 'Waggoner'. It is no coincidence that, as England was threatened by the Spanish Armada, the translation of Waghenhaer's book (as *The Mariner's Mirror*) was entrusted to Anthony Ashley, Clerk of Elizabeth I's Privy Council; the possession of accurate sea charts was a matter of national security.

The first marine atlas of the whole world, and the first to use Mercator's projection, was produced in Italy by Robert Dudley, an exiled English nobleman, the son of Elizabeth I's favourite the Earl of Leicester. Dudley fell out of favour with Elizabeth's successor James I, and moved to Florence, where he became naval advisor to the Grand Duke of Tuscany. The one hundred and thirty charts in his *Dell'Arcano del Mare* (1646-7) are all based on original surveys rather than copied from existing maps. This monumental work remained unsurpassed for half a century until Louis XIV's minister Colbert commissioned an official naval survey. The resulting atlas, *Le Neptune François*, was published by the French royal geographer Alexis-Hubert Jaillot in Paris in 1693.

If intellectual curiosity drove the exploration of the seas and skies, so too did the commercial and imperial ambitions of Portugal, Spain, and later Holland, England and France, whose mariners scoured the oceans in search of cod, furs, whales, and a northwest or northeast passage to the fabled riches of the Orient. The Elizabethan mathematician William Bourne spelled out the economic benefits plainly:

> It is not vnknowne how necessarie Nauigation is, both for the transportation of our commodities, to find vent for them in other countries (whereby no small number of people is set a worke in England) and also the bringing of other commodities (that we have neede of) vnto vs, by which meanes the Queenes Maiestie receyueth no small benefit for hir customes . . .

One problem continued to challenge scientists and navigators, however. To determine longitude, it is necessary to establish local time by the position of the sun or other celestial bodies and compare it with the time at the prime meridian. Since no one had yet made a clock that would remain accurate over the duration of a lengthy sea voyage, it remained impossible to establish precise longitude over great distances, and mariners remained dependent on unreliable lunar calculations. In 1658, the Dutch astronomer Christiaan Huygens attempted to design a pendulum clock that would work at sea. Robert Hooke tested it, but found that the rocking of the ship disrupted the action of the pendulum. To overcome this, he proposed a pocket watch driven by a hairspring, but his idea was not developed.

The problem was considered so intractable that in 1714 the British Parliament established a Board of Longitude and offered a prize of £20,000 for its solution, but it was not until 1759, after several attempts, that the London clockmaker John Harrison succeeded in creating an accurate, portable 'sea watch' or marine chronometer.

The measurement of latitude, meanwhile, underwent significant improvement for the first time since Davis's quadrant more than a century earlier. In 1731 John Hadley invented a wooden-framed octant, which used mirrors and prisms to measure the angle of a star to the horizon, and in 1759 John Bird extended the range of the instrument from an eighth to a sixth of a circle to produce the first sextant.

The Industrial Revolution and the development of steamships led to a massive increase in commercial shipping, which demanded a corresponding improvement in marine cartography. From 1829 to 1855, under Francis Beaufort, Britain's Hydrographic Office made the Admiralty chart the world standard. In the United States, Nathaniel Bowditch's *New American Practical Navigator* first appeared in 1802, and was regularly updated (a modern edition is still in use today), while the Coast Survey, founded by Thomas Jefferson in 1807, produced high-quality charts for both government and commercial use.

Industrialisation also facilitated the mass production of precision-engineered instruments that had hitherto been expensive luxuries. The marine chronometer could now be manufactured in sufficient quantity to supplant lunar calculations in determining longitude. Hadley's octant went out of production by the middle of the nineteenth century, superseded by the sextant which, with its metal frame and longer arc, made it easier to calculate latitude.

In the twentieth century these instruments were supplemented – and to a considerable extent made obsolete – by radio signals, sonar, radar and GPS. Yet in spite of the many electronic aids now available to mariners, to qualify for a captain's licence from the US Coast Guard or the UK Maritime and Coastguard Agency it is still necessary to demonstrate competence in celestial navigation. Should a ship's computers fail, or the GPS be closed to civilian users during military exercises, mariners still look to the stars.

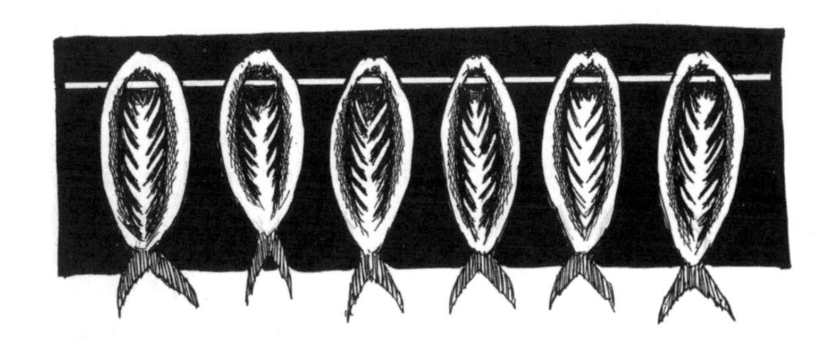

How to Smoke a Herring

Mike Smylie

First Catch Your Fish

The Great Yarmouth fish salesman John Wm De Caux tells us that the herring is to man the most valuable and, therefore, the most important fish in northern waters.[†] Loch Fyne and the surrounding area was of course long renowned for the quality and abundance of its herring, swimming in shoals many miles long and two across: 'from Kenmore south to Saddell Bay the blind shoals wander in the sea/I ply my spade and watch them play – God, what is it but mockery?' [‡]

Loch Fyne was where the ring net was born. In the early 1830s some Tarbert fishermen experimented with a seine net sent out from the shore with a single small skiff and set around a shoal. Soon two skiffs were being sent out with a net between them to encircle the shoal. The results were spectacular – so spectacular, indeed, that legislation forced through by the traditional drift-net fishers from up-loch banned the method. The ring-net fishermen were forced to work at night, under cover of darkness. It was

---

† *The Herring and the Herring Fishery*, 1881

‡ George Campbell Hay: 'The Fisherman Speaks' in *Wind on Loch Fyne*, 1938

a tough business. The hard-pressed fishers had to avoid being detected by patrols of soldiers; and the soldiers were not the only reason for watchfulness. The essence of success was to spot the 'natural appearances' that betrayed the presence of the shoals – the diving Solan goose, the porpoise, known to nibble at the edges of the shoals, the oil on the water, the 'fire in the water' brought on by the sea's own phosphorescence and the fishes' movement. (There is also, by the way, a good case for maintaining that herring fart. It appears that unlike any other fish, they emit bubbles from their anus. A high-pitched raspberry sound seems to be a means of communication and may help keep the shoal together. De Caux again: 'Herrings, when hauled alive, will occasionally make a slight noise . . . Some persons speak of the sound as being a kind of squeak, but it resembles a sneeze rather than a squeak. The nearest approach to the sound is the word "cheese", and that is so proved by the fact that fishermen, when they hear it, call out, "Don't sing out cheese; we want you for bread!"')

In June 1861 Peter MacDougall, a young Ardrishaig fisherman, was shot and killed by a marine and his superior officer standing watch from the shore close to Otter Spit†. In 1867 the opponents of ring-netting saw its benefits and crossed the floor, and the practice became legal.

It was once regarded a foul thing to land dead or 'mashed' herring. Aboard the skiff *Rolling Wave* it was a rush to get the brailer out to get the herring into the hold.

> For there is a terrible heaviness in dead herring at the bottom of the net. They cast off the tow and their neighbour came round to the net and began to brail them out and into her own hold, with the great cone-shaped brailer swinging out on the yard and in again, and the cod end opened over the open hatchway so that they slid out flipping and slithering and all colours, pink and green and blue, but all with the silver

† Angus Martin: *The Ring-Net Fishermen*, 1981

> brightness through them . . . 'Fine fishing in her, boys!' 'Three hundred baskets anyway.' 'Aye, and that more!'†

Immerse in a Strong Solution of Brine

Salting herring has two benefits: firstly, it draws out moisture from the fish, which helps preservation; and secondly, it helps kill off almost all types of bacteria and fungi.

The practice is by no means confined to herring, though millions of barrels of salt herring were exported around the globe in the nineteenth and very early twentieth century. Salt herring were never popular in Britain, though salt cod and salted pilchards were once regularly seen (preferably from a safe distance).

Vast numbers of British-caught herrings 'go foreign' (to use the Yarmouth expression) salted and packed in barrels, salt fish being little, if at all, eaten in Britain. On 13 March 1917, Captain Bathurst, MP, answering Mr Watts, MP, in the House of Commons, stated that the quantity of herrings pickled in brine in Stornoway alone was 75,000 barrels, and, although its export was prohibited, there was no demand in this country for this particular kind of fish, which was very cheap and good food; he himself had eaten some of these very pickled herrings, and desired nothing better.‡

A word of warning about brining in the correct way. Samuel again:

> Of the salt itself more will be said; Professor Hutchinson, some years ago, had a word to say about the connection between unsound salt fish and leprosy, but in these days of ample vegetable supplies we need not think twice about recommending the use of good salt fish for habitual consumption among our fellow countrymen. Sound and well cured, it is as safe as fresh fish, but fish carelessly salted deteriorates easily and quickly becomes unsound, and is held responsible by some authorities for leprosy in Scandinavia, on the south coast of Africa, and elsewhere.

---

† Mitchison & Macintosh: *Men and Herring*, 1949

‡ A M Samuel: *The Herring*, 1918

The herring lassies in the nineteenth and early twentieth century, free from leprosy and expert at the preparation of cured herring, were a phenomenon never to be repeated in British history. Coming in the main from Scottish families, they travelled the country following the fishing fleets. Starting from Lerwick in Shetland, they descended southwards in droves on specially-chartered trains or, later, buses, to their accommodation in the various ports, usually ending up at Lowestoft or Great Yarmouth for the great autumn fishery.

Something like 900 million herring were caught [in 1861] and much of this fish was landed into Wick, on the northeastern extremity of the country. The following year some 50 million herring were gutted by 3500 herring lassies over a two-day period and more than 800,000 barrels of herring were cured in total that year.†

This annual migration lasted for almost a century. At its peak there were 6000 women on the move. The speed at which they worked was incredible: in 1913, at the peak of the fishery, they cured some 854 million herring in just fourteen weeks. Generally they gutted sixty fish a minute – one a second – using a twist of the knife to remove gills and innards in one deft movement. It was an arduous and unforgiving job; but the lassies were renowned for their singing and general positive attitude.

Drip Dry and Smoke

Having been left in brine for a time that will become evident only with experience – about forty-five minutes seems right to me – the split herrings are pinned with nails through the bodies just below the heads on to tenterhooks, and left to drip dry for about an hour. This is an important part of the process, as it allows a glaze to set upon the fish, which contributes to a perfect smoking – sweet-tasting, not too salty, firm-fleshed, with a good oil and moisture content. They are then taken into the smokehouse.

---

† M Smylie: Herring – *A History of the Silver Darlings*, 2004

Place in Smokehouse for a Number of Hours . . .

The time being judged purely by the finished colour of the product that is desired; I smoke mine for, on average, sixteen hours. There are two main ways of smoking a fish – hot smoking and cold smoking. Hot smoking is the easy option – fast seafood, even if there are many seasoned sailors and land lubbers who will declare their undying passion for an Arbroath smokie, which is a hot-smoked haddock (Finnan haddies are the cold-smoked version). Cold smoking gives the finest taste; but for cold smoking you need an oily fish. The herring fits this bill perfectly. They smoke in a variety of ways, each giving a succulent yet subtle flavour. Cold smoking is a very simple procedure – which may explain why so little smoking myth and custom has been handed down through the generations.

There are no fundamental proofs as to when man first smoked his fish. There is, however, some evidence that by the Stone Age fish was being preserved in an organised fashion. Smoke would have helped keep the flies off drying fish, and it cannot have been long before our forebears realised that the smoke itself acted as a preservative. Dried, salted and smoked fish were widely eaten in Sumer in southern Mesopotamia, and a trade in dried fish had been established between settlements on the Persian Gulf in around 4000BC.[†]

In Britain in more recent times, salted and smoked fish were cheaper than fresh fish, largely due to the expensive forms of transport required by fresh fish. Cured fish could spend months in transit and arrive in the same state as when it had left. In 1298 red herrings were twenty a penny while fresh herrings were six a penny at Michaelmas and half that price after.[‡]

It is said that Yarmouth contributed much to the smoking of herring in the fourteenth century, when the red herring was being perfected. Smoking the fish had been around a long time

† C L Cutting: *Fish Saving*, 1955

‡ L F Salzman: *English Industries in the Middle Ages*, 1923

before that. In 1230 an ordinance shows that one or more trees (presumably oaks, as oak sawdust is traditionally the smoker's favourite) were given to the poor by the Abbey of Fécamp to smoke herrings. An English will of 1349 mentions a 'black house used for smoking "black" herrings'. Black herrings were the hardest dried herrings, almost leathery in texture. Red herrings were the favourite – heavily salted and well smoked. Indeed it has been said that they were left in the smokehouse for a couple of weeks at the very top so that they would lose moisture in between normal smokings before another batch of more lightly-smoked herrings were hung.

In his *Lenten Stuffe* (1599) the Lowestoft-born Thomas Nashe waxed lyrical about the red herring:

> The puissant red herring, the golden Hesperides red herring, the Meonian red herring, the red herring of Red Herrings . . . St Denis for France, St Iames for Spaine, St Patrike for Ireland, St George for England and the red herring for Yarmouth . . . A red herring is wholesome on a frosty morning: it is most precious merchandise because it can be carried through all Europe. No where are they so well cured as at Yarmouth. The poorer sort make it three parts of their sustenance . . . A red herring drawn on the ground will lead hounds a false scent.

Red herrings were not confined to East Anglia, as Daniel Defoe found in Dunbar, one of the largest ports in Scotland, in 1724. Here was a great herring fishery where herrings were smoked,

> as they do in Yarmouth in Norfolk. . . I cannot say they are cur'd so well as at Yarmouth, that is to say, not for keeping and sending on long voyages, as to Venice and Leghorn, though with a quick passage, they might hold it there too.

The smokers of the Isle of Man were also attempting to outdo the Norfolk smokers.

Golden and silver herrings take their colour from the length of their smoking. Greeks liked the golden variety – in the 1920s, after the influx of folk from Asia Minor, the open-air cinemas were aflame with golden herring wrapped in newspaper – literally; the herring-eaters set the newspaper alight, which cooked the fish (I've cooked salmon the same way in Finland). A bar in Athens still serves the fiendishly salty delicacy, washed down with volumes of tsipouro or ouzo. Silvers were popular in Italy.

Yarmouth is also renowned for its bloaters, the name coming from the Swedish *blota* (soaking or steeping) referring to the brining before smoking. A bloater – probably the most lightly-smoked form of herring – is smoked whole, ungutted and (hopefully) with the roe inside. They were first exported to Spain and Italy around 1600. Today a bloater is a rare creature indeed, though they can still be found (sometimes in my smokehouse!).

Then there's the kipper, said to have originated in Seahouses in 1843. A certain John Woodger was experimenting with salmon when he discovered the kipper by mistake (though not too much credence should be given to this story, as smoked fish often carry legends about their accidental discovery, most of which turn out to be apocryphal). It seems reasonable to assume that it was Woodger who devised the technique of splitting the fish down the back and opening it up so the belly acts as a hinge.

Once in the smokehouse, kippers-in-the-making are given (by me, anyway; practice varies in different parts of the UK) a good sixteen hours smoking over oak sawdust. Some smokers experiment with fruit woods. I don't – though I do have a bag of chestnut sawdust lurking in my cellar. This produces the golden brown colour associated with a fine (or even Loch Fyne) kipper. All that's left is to say that they are best eaten immediately, fresh out of the smoker, oil-dripping and scented, with a glass of good country cider (or strong black coffee if it's too early). If you must heat your kipper up, submerge it for a couple of minutes – no longer – in a jug of boiling water.

Scilly Pioneers

Amanda Martin

For as long as photography has existed, magazines, travel documentaries, ethnographic studies and popular fiction have been pummelling us with images of island communities around the world. The Isles of Scilly are no exception to this fascination, and indeed can claim an unusually complete pictorial record from the mid-nineteenth century onwards. Scilly's first intrepid photographers were consumed by their urge to log (and occasionally embellish) the life and events of the archipelago in all its weathers and sea states. Many excellent examples of nineteenth and early twentieth century photography are still in the islands; but the remaining collections are vulnerable to the imperial ambitions of mainland institutions, as was demonstrated by the recent Sotheby's sale of the Gibson shipwreck archive to the National Maritime Museum at Greenwich. The original archive has now been irrevocably diminished by the loss of these images.

One of the first Scillonians to try his hand at photography was John Gibson (1827-1920). Born on Inishmore, the largest of the Aran Islands in Galway Bay, he came to live in Scilly aged twelve on the death of his father James Gibson, a St Martin's man. His widowed mother ran a shop. Typically for a Scillonian lad seeking to bolster the family finances, John went to sea; but his real passport to financial security was his camera, an exotic luxury in Victorian times. He acquired his first photographic apparatus abroad. By the time he was in his mid-thirties, he could afford to open a photography studio in Penzance and move his young family to the mainland. In the 1860s the lure of the islands drew them back to Scilly, where with his sons Alexander Gendall Gibson (1857-1944) and Herbert John Gibson (1861-1937) he founded the Lyonnesse photography studio on St Mary's.

The Gibson brothers revealed very different temperaments. Alexander was a flamboyant character in dress and personality, a capable watercolourist and an obsessive autodidact who revelled in books, archaeology, architecture and folk history. He gradually came to dominate the family business, taking vast numbers of photographs of wrecks, touristic views, flower growers, archaeological sites, buildings and artefacts, not only in Scilly but all over Cornwall and beyond. An advertisement invited visitors to see his private museum of local discoveries at the Church Street house. (Some of its contents now form part of the Isles of Scilly Museum collections.) With his brother he produced a guidebook extolling the beauties of Scilly, promoting their photos and shop, and above all proclaiming their knowledge and love of the islands.

By the 1880s artists had established colonies in St Ives and Newlyn. Like most of the photographers working in the region, the Gibsons were influenced by the painters' choices of subject. Alexander realised the immense overlap between art and photography, occasionally 'improving' photos by introducing people, adding sails to a windmill or clouds to seascapes. In life and photography Alexander was a masterly teller of stories – sometimes tall ones – and creator of atmospheres. Group photos in all manner of settings were his forte. From studio family portraits to harvest festivals, via ships' crews and flower packers, Alexander's attention to detail guaranteed that every profile, skirt fold or stony look was included for a reason. His uncommissioned (and therefore unpaid) study of *A House in Blood Alley, Hugh Town* (c. 1898) reveals him as a social commentator. The scene has been carefully staged: a babe in arms, two young children staring straight into the camera, a mother partially visible in the doorway. Such images of poor Scillonians are at odds with the laborious studio shots of the affluent middle class that maintained the Gibson family livelihood in Scilly and in Penzance. Posterity has accorded huge importance to the large number of photographs recording wrecks around the coasts of Cornwall and Scilly; but the truly memorable images are of people: gravediggers, passengers, schoolchildren and family groups.

Herbert Gibson's quiet steadiness made him the perfect foil for Alexander's exuberance. A good businessman and an able photographer, Herbert's photographic legacy has been almost entirely engulfed by the dominating character of his older brother. In the book *Island Camera*, the family's tribute to itself published in 1972, a mere ten photos bear his name; but they include some of the images that we know best today. His eye for the important details of history led him into the Western Rocks. In his image of the re-casing of the Bishop Rock Lighthouse in 1887, workmen can be seen shuffling around the column on a narrow granite ledge, laboriously lifting, dragging and fitting the huge granite blocks that constitute the second skin. Hauling his precious camera onto Rosevear, a small, barren island near Bishop Rock, he photographed the ruins of the buildings (*On Rosevear*, c. 1890) that housed the lighthouse builders.

Herbert may be scarcely remembered nowadays, but his contemporary reputation was as great as his brother's. When Alexander Gibson accepted the Gorsedd's invitation to become a Bard of Honour (Father of the Islands), Tas an Enesow, the Grand Bard said:

> had your brother lived you may take it that the recognition we gladly give to you would have included him also, who was

> so closely connected with you in the good work of discovery and recording the ancient things of the Islands and West Cornwall.

It is largely thanks to Herbert's influence that the business aspect of their photography survived and thrived. His enthusiasm for photographing shipwrecks continued years after the more 'artistic' Alexander had lost interest.

Surprisingly, two other notable photographers were active in Scilly over several decades: Charles J King (c. 1858-1939), known as C J King, and Francis J Mortimer (1874-1944).

A native of Southend-on-Sea and a trained dispenser, C J King came to Scilly in 1890 to open the first St Mary's pharmacy. An early interest in photography soon became an absorbing passion. In 1894, it became legal to manufacture and distribute picture postcards, which could be sent through the post. King seized this opportunity and made the first picture postcards to be sold in the islands.

'Fudgy' King was a keen all-round sportsman, playing water polo and swimming in the sea throughout the year. This stood him in good stead as he became increasingly enthusiastic about wildlife photography. He pioneered the stalking and photographing of wild seabirds and seals, hauling his cumbersome plate cameras up the most perilous of rocks, building elaborate temporary hides. Islanders wondered at Mr King's vigils in his precariously perched hideouts. On one occasion he spent many hours on Castle Bryher, a tiny islet in the Norrard Rocks, in order to photograph some peregrine falcons' nests and young.

In the first edition of the *Scillonian Magazine*, the chronicle of the life and people of the isles of Scilly that has been in continuous production since 1925, he wrote movingly of his passion:

> . . . in these Islands of the West we have a perfect paradise for the Amateur Photographer. The writer has during the last thirty odd years had the opportunity for taking a camera of

> one kind or another into many parts of England and the Continent, but he can safely say that in no district has he found so many possibilities for good and interesting work, confined in a similar space, as in our Islands of Scilly . . .
>
> Not only is this wealth of subjects available, but the conditions are unusually favourable, for in no other place in Great Britain is the active power of the light equal to that of Scillonia. Here with a good lens of wide aperture snapshots may be taken all through the winter, and even with the cheaper class of cameras which are now so popular, good work may be done during at least eight months of the year. Indeed many amateurs, who come to Scilly and start work without asking for local advice, find when they develop their first roll of films or their first packet of plates that they have over-exposed them.

In old age he returned to live in Essex but continued to give lectures all over the country on the bird life of Scilly.

Known to his family as 'F J', Francis J Mortimer was brought up in Portsmouth. The scion of a St Agnes family, he went on to gain an international reputation as a photographer but always regarded Scilly as a second home. A pioneer of the bromoil process, which gave a soft, paint-like quality to prints, and well known for his dramatic seascapes, he was adamant that photography should be recognised as an art form.

With his homemade waterproof camera and clothing, F J would clamber over rocky headlands and set sail during rough seas to photograph wild storms and vessels in distress. Describing big-wave hunting in the islands in the spring of 1902, F J told a reporter:

> The Sea has many times carried away my apparatus as the spoils of victory. I stand on a rock just out of reach and watch wave after wave roll in, each breaking at a certain point. The next is a monster that smashes on my rock and I'm lucky to escape alive. Never turn your back on the sea for an instant.

> The last time I did that put me to bed for a week with bruises and smashed camera.

An atmospheric series of black and white photographs, some taken by Mortimer, some arranged by him for others to take, reveal his fascination with Scillonian breakers. F J himself can be seen at the edge of turbulent seas clutching his cumbersome camera, waiting for the right moment to press the shutter.

Other anecdotes from his 1902 diary tell of medical emergencies 'May 11th F J went to the Gugh. Then William George was taken ill so they sailed across to St Mary's for a doctor and had to row him back', trips out to the lighthouses,'May 12th Georgie loaded a boat for the Bishop Rock . . . able to land at the lighthouse and had a good sail back. F J got knocked on the head by a block, but managed to take some flashlights . . . On May 13th set off in the gig for Round Island (first calling in at St Mary's for drinks at the Atlantic)', wave hunting 'out to Peninnis for wave pictures', and storm watching 'May 13th drenched again in North West gales, May 17th proved a real N West storm. F J wet through in squall.' But always his camera and its processes are omnipresent. 'May 19th. . . changed thirty plates in a little bedroom with two blankets over the window.'

Mortimer kept detailed photo diaries; he logged local activities such as the crowning of the May Queen, work at the Marconi station, visiting Tresco Abbey, sailing in Hell Bay and the lifting of kelp. He would stay up until the early hours of the morning developing and changing the half-plate glass negatives. In March 1911, F J took the last picture of the lighted lamp at St Agnes Lighthouse.

His wider portfolio included Dutch scenes, naval training and patriotic British World War I home front images. Through his editorship of *Amateur Photographer & Photography* (1908-1944) and *Photograms of the Year* (1912-1944) he made the case that photography was an art form, championing the large amateur photographic societies of his day.

Mortimer favoured manipulated image techniques such as the bromoil process and composite negatives. Proponents of 'purist' negative-perfect photography dismissed such methods as print-making mimicry. A photo portrait of Mortimer shows a genial dreamer. In Scilly F J was part of the great St Agnes Mortimer clan, known for joining in with all the chores and outings, yet beyond the islands his stature was great. In May 1992 the Camera Club drew from its permanent collection to exhibit a panel of his work. Entitled *Sail Ho!*, it included photographs of ships at war, working vessels and leisure craft, many of them taken in situations where movement was hard to freeze, considering the limitations of film emulsion speeds of the day. The photographs are an important record of the role of maritime pursuits within British life in the 1930s and '40s.

Until his death in 1944, Mortimer remained an enthusiastic communicator of new developments in photography, still photographing what were to him essentially timeless subjects – the sea and its traditions.

The Gibson brothers, King and Mortimer shared a tremendous love of the Isles of Scilly. Alexander, Herbert and F J were integral to the community, family men, craftsmen, employers, founder contributors to the *Scillonian Magazine,* involved at every level, whereas Francis was a part-time Scillonian whose professional reputation was known across the world. The island-based photographers had to balance the constraints of earning a living from tourists, running various local businesses and dealing with making time to take photographs and keep abreast of new developments in photography. These very different men had in common an obsessive enthusiasm for recording the world around them. In spite of their ponderous equipment and the difficult conditions in which they used it, their ingenuity, courage and almost unhealthy stubbornness enabled them to produce a formidable, not to say unique, record of their time and place.

Salmo

Martin Llewellyn

Spring is arriving in the northern hemisphere. The snows are retreating to their mountainous summer refuges. Icicles sparkle prettily, and the drip of the meltwater becomes a roaring flood. In the headwaters of rivers that flow into the North Atlantic, among shallow rapids and tumbled stones, hundreds of thousands of small, dark-speckled fish are undergoing a radical transformation. Longer, warmer days are triggering cascades of corticosteroids in their forefinger-long bodies. A kind of accelerated adolescence ensues; in a few weeks they will be big-eyed silver smolt, recognisable as juvenile salmon, streaking downstream at twenty-five kilometres a day, tiny but enthusiastic teleosts ploughing forwards and out into the open sea.

Henry Williamson and a host of other authors have taken us up rivers with salmon, but we have little by way of familiar imagery about their lives at sea. Here there are no death-defying leaps up foaming waterfalls, no gentle swishing of fly rods on late summer afternoons. Instead, the silent vastness of the salty brown-blue deep, thousands of kilometres of it, torn by currents, underslung with abyssal chasms and mighty mountain ranges. Understanding what Atlantic salmon do in this wilderness – where they migrate, what they eat, how they navigate, and what triggers their return – is of crucial importance. The clouds of smolts that dash from river mouths in late spring are as numerous as they ever were. Mysteriously, however, fewer and fewer actually return as adults to spawn.

On a cold summer morning in Maniitsoq on the West Coast of Greenland, Agdluak is heading out to check his nets. It is mid-July, and Agdluak, woolly hat jammed down on his head and thick orange parka zipped up tight, is hunched behind the steering post of his small blue skiff. The sixty-horsepower Mercury howls between snow-blotched headlands that slant suddenly into white-capped waves on a blue-green sea. Chunks of ice still drift about. It is properly cold. Rounding the point, Agdluak throttles back in the shelter of a small cove. With a turn of speed for a fat man, he leaps forward and plucks a faded orange buoy from the water. As he hauls the monofilament net, great silvery-blue shapes materialise and rise towards him in the dark water. They are salmon, fat as butter, the shape of overfed torpedoes, the best part of a metre long.

Salmon caught off the West Greenland coastline are usually in their second or third year at sea. They come inshore in summer to feed in waters teeming with krill, amphipods, capelin and squid. The red carotenoid pigments of their crustacean prey accumulate in their tissues. Thousands of miles away, when they spawn, degrading muscle releases those same molecules into their skin, which blossoms into the sunburst of colour that will help them attract a mate.

The oceanic feeding grounds of Atlantic Salmon were discovered as recently as the mid-1950s. A commercial fishery was founded, boomed, and went just about bust in the space of twenty years. The monsters that Agdluak has pulled over the side, now neatly gutted in two fish boxes in the stern of his boat, are part of a small subsistence catch. Destined for a squat market building near the quay, they will lie in neat lines alongside great slabs of dark whale meat and chunks of ivory-white narwhal blubber. The reduction of the Greenland Atlantic Salmon fishery represents a major feat of international cooperation, and has almost certainly brought the species back from the brink – though it is hard not to sympathise with the Greenlanders, who have lost precious export income. After all, it was not Greenland-owned ships laying kilometres of drift nets in the late 1970s.

Scientists have taken years to reach a consensus as to how a tiny smolt, perhaps only a year old and hardly as big as a sardine, can, after only eighteen months, weigh more than twenty kilos, and be chasing squid at depths of up to two hundred metres.

Some Atlantic salmon populations, like those in Labrador and north Norway, make only modest migrations into the near-by ocean. In Russia, a few populations never reach the ocean at all, passing their lives in and around Lake Ladoga, just west of St Petersburg. But the vast majority swim seawards as smolts until they reach the great vortex of the North Atlantic subpolar gyre – a huge merry-go-round of interlocking currents, the Labrador, Irminger, and West Greenland among them, which carries the juvenile fish anticlockwise around the Northern Atlantic.

Smolts and post-smolts are epipelagic, swimming and feeding less than a hundred metres beneath the surface. They are also, unfortunately for them, largely passive, at the mercy of currents and predators human and otherwise. Those that don't end up in the stomach of a whale (as pop-up satellite tags attest), or as the by-catch of purse seiners (they are easily missed among a huge shoal of mackerel), might make it to feeding grounds of the Faroe Islands, where one-sea-winter fish are found. The long-term fate of the Atlantic salmon will almost certainly be determined by what happens to smolts and post-smolts in international fishing grounds, which even if they escape predation are reliant on currents whose paths are made increasingly unpredictable by climate change.

The survivors grow to become large and powerful fish. Once they have attained sexual maturity, which takes between one and three years, adult salmon leave the gyre, heading for their natal river. For a short time, Atlantic salmon join the ranks of the great migrants of the ocean, out-pacing even bluefin tuna at over a hundred kilometres a day. They stop feeding, and all that hard-won protein and fat is set to the single-minded pursuit of home.

Open ocean travel seems to be guided by magnetism, currents and polarising light. Closer in, the search along the coastline for the estuary that will lead them back into fresh water seems to be guided by smell. And there we are back in the land of poetry, with Henry Williamson and Salar the Salmon hunting for the unique chemical signal that will send him racing upstream:

> At Full Moon the tides swirling over the Island Race carry the feelings of many rivers to the schools of fish that have come in from their feeding ledges of the deep Atlantic. The returning salmon are excited and confused. Under the broken waters the moon's glimmer is opalescent; the fish swim up from the ocean's bed, and leap to meet the sparkling silver which lures and ever eludes them . . .†

So the circle, though increasingly fragile, is unbroken.

---

† From *Salar the Salmon* by Henry Williamson, Little Toller Books, 2010

From the Editor's Shelf

The shelves seem to be filling up with books about fishing at roughly the same speed as the fish are being hauled out of the sea, which means quickly. First to hand are some excellent and beautifully-illustrated specimens from Mike Smylie, MQ contributor, master kipper smoker, and all-round expert. He has embarked on a six-book series called 'The Fishing Industry Through Time'. The first two, *The Tweed to the Northern Isles* and *From Duncansby Head to the Solway Firth* (Amberley, £14.99) will be followed by three more this year. Each book has sections on fishing methods, boats, people, and settlements. The photographs are not far short of miraculous, and the narrative, as one would expect from Smylie, is crisp and authoritative. A highly collectable series, worthy of a shelf of its own – and worth reinforcing with the same author's *Traditional Fishing Boats of Europe* and *Traditional Fishing Boats of Britain* (Amberley, £19.99).

East coast traditional boat enthusiasts will enjoy *East Coast Oysters and a Few Whelks*, a book of black and white photographs and a little text by Mervyn Maggs (Jardine Press, £12). It is full of beautiful photographs of boats, people, shellfish and marshscapes. The bracing aroma of salt mud and oysters rolls out of the page, and will bring a nostalgic tear to the eye of anyone who has ever sailed by the low land under the vast skies of the east of England.

Lodestar Books, a reliable source of excellent small-boat literature revivals, has published two books calculated (at £12 each) to gratify the growing numbers of sail-and-oar enthusiasts. First is Conor O'Brien's *Sea-Boats, Oars and Sails,* first published in 1941. The title pretty much sums up the book, but not the views of its author – a gun-runner, intellectual, circumnavigator and all-purpose tough egg – which are sometimes interesting and useful, sometimes idiosyncratic, and occasionally (as in his advocacy of carvel building for the home shipwright) plain misguided. But O'Brien is a man with whom it is a pleasure to disagree, and the book is much brightened by fine moody photographs of an elegant boat designed by Francois Vivier, the sail-and-oar king of France.

Next comes *Sail and Oar: drawings of Yorkshire's North Sea Fishery before the advent of steam* by Ernest Dade, a pupil of the artist-yachtsman Albert Strange. The drawings of smacks, yawls and cobles are elegant, and the information conveyed in the captions is fascinating. Until I saw this book I had no idea how a steam trawler towed a fishing coble (stern first, as it happens, the towline never made fast but grimly hung on to by the coble's crew). Full of ideas, dodges and wheezes for summer testing.

For rainy days, there is Sophia Kingshill and Jennifer Westwood's *The Fabled Coast: a compendium of legends and traditions from around the shores of Britain and Ireland* (Random House, £20). The authors display huge erudition, lightly worn, in analysing myths familiar (the Kraken, Drake's Drum) and less familiar (the discovery of America by the Welsh). A handy addition to the boat's bookshelf, useful as a continuous read, a reference book and (in extreme circumstances, during encounters with monsters of the deep) a field guide.

Empire of the Deep: the rise and fall of the British Navy by Ben Wilson (Orion, £25) does exactly what it says on the packet, and is an efficient medium-length (at six hundred and fifty pages) history. Personally, I will be waiting for the third and final volume in N A M Rodger's magisterial Naval History of Britain, due to be published in 2015. Anyone who has not read the first two volumes

– *The Safeguard of the Sea* and *The Command of the Ocean* (both Penguin, £20) – should put this right without delay.

Sam Llewellyn

Collins Bird Guide (£19.99)
Collins Complete Guide to British Birds (£16.99)
RSPB Handbook of British Birds (Christopher Helm, £9.99)
RSPB Pocket Guide to British Birds (A & C Black, £6.99)

The Field Guide to Birds of Britain and Europe (Collins, 1954), by Roger Tory Peterson, Guy Mountfort, and P A D Hollom, was Europe's definitive bird bible for fifty years. Its purpose was to foster 'the enjoyment of birds, whether casual or absorbing, which man has developed during centuries of sentimental attachment'.

So what of modern guides?

In July 2013 I packed the *Collins Bird Guide*, the photographic *Collins Complete Guide to British Birds*, the *RSPB Handbook of British Birds*, and the more recent *RSPB Pocket Guide to British Birds*, and headed north.

The plan was to sail to St Kilda from Stornoway on a friend's boat. A forty-mile cruise down the east coast of Lewis and Harris followed by fifty miles of open sea would give the bird books a useful workout.

As I waited on Stornoway quay with my kitbag, my mobile phone rang. A crackly voice said, 'The weather's rubbish. Join us for a sail round Shetland?'

As I went ashore at Papa Stour, I was attacked by flocks of terns. The common tern has a black tipped orange-red bill, the arctic tern a uniformly blood-red bill, but neither beak is easy to identify if (like me) you are one of the eight per cent of men who are partially colour-blind. Further on I saw numerous small brown birds (SBBs) perched on fence posts. It was time to test the books.

The *Collins Bird Guide* is too comprehensive, with one hundred and fifty pages and nine hundred illustrations of small brown birds. I therefore turned to the Collins photographic *Complete Guide to British Birds,* which offered a more limited choice of one hundred pages of SBBs, illustrated with four hundred photographs. Even to start identification you need to choose the right chapter. The *RSPB Pocket Guide to British Birds* required the same level of triage. I gave up.

Next morning, as we motorsailed along the cold bleak west cliffs of Shetland, I became increasingly confused and dispirited. We landed. At Lerwick Tourist Centre I picked up an RSPB A3 poster, reassuringly entitled *Birds you might see in Orkney and Shetland,* and the slim, full-colour *Birds of a Shetland Summer* showing thirty-four species in a hundred and thirty pages of beautiful photographs. It was time to take on board some local knowledge.

So next day I joined fifteen bird lovers on Dr Jonathan Wills's *Dunter III* at the Victoria Pier. As we rounded Score Head the huge cliffs of Noss Head came into sight. Wheeling gulls and diving gannets filled the air and the sea was alive with bobbing guillemots, razorbills, gulls and puffins.

I pulled out my books. 'That's the Bible,' remarked a friendly twitcher, seeing Svensson's *Collins Bird Guide.* I opened it at the gannet page. Svensson writes: 'Makes stunning steep diagonal dives for fish from a height of 10-40m, wings thrown back just prior to striking the surface.'

The photographic *Collins Complete Guide to British Birds* tends towards more complete, lyrical sentences. In its gannets section it says, 'When a shoal of fish is discovered groups of birds plunge dive from a great height, providing an extraordinary spectacle.' For the partially colour-blind, a photographic guide conveys absolute authenticity.

By comparison the RSPB guides seem confusing, condescending and earnest. The watercolours are scattered about the pages in illogical sizes, in illogical positions, so it is difficult to compare species. Graphic designers rather than ornithologists have laid out their pages. These books are liable to stoke arguments rather than settle them.

As I gaze at the pile of books in front of me, I return inevitably to a small hardback lying beside them. It is bound in modest blue buckram, a gold-blocked hoopoe pressed into its spine. It is a 1954 first edition of *A Field Guide to the Birds of Britain and Europe*, and it carries me back to a time when the amateur study of birds was understood to emanate from 'sentimental attachment'. Like mine.

Alex Dufort

A lot of books about battleships and similar
Various publishers, terrible dear

I bet the reason they are putting out all them battleship books is because it is the hundredth anniversary of the First World War. I was in that, did you know? In the old *Tobacco Trader*, off the beach. Funny to think of it now, really. Young chaps nowadays don't know they've been born. Let them sit on the *Tobacco Trader* as referred to above, buying cheap fags off of the pongoes at fair prices and getting dive bombed. Unparalleled First World War business opportunity, Dunkirk –

Ray?

What is it?

Dunkirk was in 1940. The Second World War. And you weren't there.

Do I still get paid?

Unlikely. Oh, all right. If you go away.

As told to the MQ by Ray Doggett
Master, MV *Tobacco Trader*

CONTRIBUTORS

Commodore Fraser Fraser-Harris (1916-2003) was an outstanding Fleet Air Arm fighter pilot during the Second World War. After the War he became Assistant Chief of Naval Staff before moving to the Caribbean to skipper the Baltic ketch *Ring Andersen*. *John Clegg* was skipper of the 12-metre *Flica* in the same waters at the same time.

Bob Harris is the son of Harry Harris, one of the last of the Thames lightermen to 'drive under oars'.

Ralph Hammond Innes (1913-1998) remains one of Britain's greatest thriller writers. An enthusiastic yachtsman, his experiences at sea informed many of his novels.

John Lang has served in both the Merchant and Royal Navies. After leaving the Navy he was the United Kingdom's Chief Inspector of Marine Accidents. He is currently President of the Association of Sail Training Organisations.

Martin Llewellyn is a molecular epidemiologist. After ten years at the London School of Hygiene and Tropical Medicine, he is a recent convert to the world of fish and marine systems. He is currently building the first full picture of an Atlantic Salmon's microbiome.
http://populationsofpestilentparasites.wordpress.com/

Amanda Martin is the Curator of the Isles of Scilly Museum, an Associate Member of the Museums Association of Great Britain and a freelance translator and editor. Her new booklet *Viewing the Past: the Photographic Heritage of the Isles of Scilly* is due out this spring.

Emma Beynon was born in Rhossili and learned to sail off the Gower. Time spent off the sea is dedicated to Open Ground, an exciting new venture in teaching writing to all comers in outdoor space.
www.opengroundwriting.co.uk

Alastair Robertson is a journalist specialising in Aberdeen and its hinterland, Scottish politics and the politics, fisheries and ecology of the North Sea.

Christopher Schüler is a freelance writer, journalist and editor specialising in literature, travel and the arts. His books include three histories of cartography.
www.cjschuler.com

Nigel Sharp is a lifelong sailor who owns a 1963 Nordic Folkboat and a share in an 1898 Falmouth Working Boat. For thirty-five years he worked in the British boatbuilding industry, and since 2010 has been pursuing a career as a freelance marine writer and photographer.

John Simpson grew up on the north shore of the Thames estuary. Early voyages on his father's smack generated a lifetime's passion for sailing and the sea.

Mike Smylie is the author of many books on historic fishing subjects. As 'Kipperman', he extols the virtues of the herring and its history, as well as demonstrating his mobile smokehouse. He lives between Bristol and a mountain village in Central Greece.

COVER ARTISTS

FRONT: *Herbert Barnard John Everett* 1876-1949

John Everett (he did not like being called Herbert) was born in Dorset. He studied painting at the Slade, and early demonstrated a passion for the sea which went further than merely painting it. He signed on as a working member of the crew of the Sydney-bound barque *Iquique* in 1898, and made fifteen other voyages.

He maintained his enthusiasm for marine subjects throughout his life. He seems to have been particularly fascinated by the 'dazzle camouflage' pioneered by Norman Wilkinson, designed to break up ships' outlines. He was not the only one: the vorticist Edward Wadsworth supervised the painting of 2000 ships, while Picasso maintained that it was the Cubists who had invented it. Whatever the truth, dazzle camouflage seems to have been more decorative than effective. It did, however, inspire some beautiful paintings, of which *A Cunarder being converted to a Merchant Cruiser* is one of the finest. (It is perhaps unnecessary to note that no Cunarder ever was in fact converted to a merchant cruiser.)

BACK: *Detail from the 'Tabula Rogeriana', Muhammad al-Idrisi*

The *Tabula Rogeriana* – the Book of Roger, so called because it was compiled at the court of Roger II, the Norman King of Sicily, in 1154 – is in fact entitled 'The book of pleasant travels into faraway lands'. Idrisi, who was born in Ceuta, where his statue now stands, was a traveller, Egyptologist and descendant of the Prophet.

The detail here, taken from a compilation of the pages of the atlas, shows a decent representation of Europe and North Africa. As was often the way with early maps, the world was depicted north downwards, and contains several extra islands in the northwest Atlantic.